T0229093

Information Protection Playbook

Information Protection Playbook

Edited by
Greg Kane
Lorna Koppel

AMSTERDAM • BOSTON • HEIDELBERG • LONDON
NEW YORK • OXFORD • PARIS • SAN DIEGO
SAN FRANCISCO • SINGAPORE • SYDNEY • TOKYO

Security
Executive Council

Elsevier
The Boulevard, Langford Lane, Kidlington, Oxford, OX5 1GB, UK
225 Wyman Street, Waltham, MA 02451, USA

First published 2013

Copyright © 2013 The Security Executive Council. Published by Elsevier Inc. All rights reserved.

No part of this publication may be reproduced or transmitted in any form or by any means, electronic or mechanical, including photocopying, recording, or any information storage and retrieval system, without permission in writing from the publisher. Details on how to seek permission, further information about the Publisher's permissions policies and our arrangement with organizations such as the Copyright Clearance Center and the Copyright Licensing Agency, can be found at our website: www.elsevier.com/permissions.

This book and the individual contributions contained in it are protected under copyright by the Publisher (other than as may be noted herein).

Notices
Knowledge and best practice in this field are constantly changing. As new research and experience broaden our understanding, changes in research methods, professional practices, or medical treatment may become necessary.

Practitioners and researchers must always rely on their own experience and knowledge in evaluating and using any information, methods, compounds, or experiments described herein. In using such information or methods they should be mindful of their own safety and the safety of others, including parties for whom they have a professional responsibility.

To the fullest extent of the law, neither the Publisher nor the authors, contributors, or editors, assume any liability for any injury and/or damage to persons or property as a matter of products liability, negligence or otherwise, or from any use or operation of any methods, products, instructions, or ideas contained in the material herein.

British Library Cataloguing in Publication Data
A catalogue record for this book is available from the British Library

Library of Congress Cataloging-in-Publication Data
A catalog record for this book is available from the Library of Congress

ISBN: 978-0-12-417232-6

For more publications in the Elsevier Risk Management and Security Collection, visit our website at store.elsevier.com/SecurityExecutiveCouncil.

This book has been manufactured using Print On Demand technology. Each copy is produced to order and is limited to black ink. The online version of this book will show color figures where appropriate.

www.elsevier.com • www.bookaid.org

Printed and bound by CPI Group (UK) Ltd, Croydon, CR0 4YY

Transferred to digital print 2013

CONTENTS

ACKNOWLEDGMENTS

The goal in creating this playbook was to provide current practices and the latest insights gathered from the collective knowledge of leading security and risk practitioners in the industry. We wish to thank everyone that made this possible by contributing their time, effort, and wisdom.

The following individuals provided assistance with the Elsevier edition of this playbook:

Herbert Mattord, Ph.D., CISM, CISSP

Michael Whitman, Ph.D., CISM, CISSP

The following individuals provided assistance with the initial version of this playbook, which was provided to the Security Executive Council community:

Michael Assante, CSO, Idaho Labs (currently at American Electric Power)

Anton Bommersbach, senior manager of global security, Wrigley (currently at Sony DADC)

Scott Day, CISO, Cargill

Greg Halvacs, DOS, Kraft (currently at Cardinal)

Bob Hayes, managing director, Security Executive Council

Stash Jarocki, senior VP and ISO, Bessemer Trust (currently at Phoenix Children's Hospital)

Kathleen Kotwica, PhD, EVP and chief knowledge strategist, Security Executive Council

Jack McCarthy, emeritus faculty, Security Executive Council, former global director of corporate security for Texaco Inc.

John McClurg, VP global security, Honeywell (currently at Dell)

Carlos Mena, CISO; vice president, program management, Security Executive Council (currently at SanDisk)

John Pontrelli, VP and CSO, Tri-West Healthcare

The *Information Protection Playbook* provides a framework and tools to create, manage, and execute all facets of an organization's information protection (IP) program. In this playbook, we guide the security leader through the development, implementation, and maintenance of a successful IP program. The playbook begins with a detailed description of the concept and value of information protection, transitioning into a step-by-step guide to building or enhancing an IP program.

Using the instructions provided in this playbook, security managers will learn how to implement the five functions of an IP framework: governance, program planning, risk management, incident response management, and program administration. This playbook also explains how the security or business leader can maintain a successful IP program in the long term. Its extensive appendices, which include sample forms, templates, and definitions, make it an excellent resource for the security manager who's building an IP program from the ground up. An abridged version of the contents of the playbook is provided in Appendix A.

WHAT IS A PLAYBOOK?

A playbook is an excellent tool for the security or business leader who wants to develop, implement, enhance, or validate a specific aspect of a security or risk management program. Playbooks provide a detailed treatment of a specific security program or service that can be quickly and effectively applied to an immediate need within an organization. Playbooks define and present the essential elements most often used by successful practitioners. They provide a framework that a security professional can use to set up, manage, and communicate the program to stakeholders. Playbooks also provide supplementary templates, forms, and checklists for immediate adaptation, and may be used by security professionals who need an introduction and plan for action on a new job responsibility, are adding a new program, or a revalidating an existing level of service. Playbooks are particularly useful for educators that are committed to providing current, relevant information and practices distilled from successful practitioners and programs and that have a direct correlation to current security positions.

ABOUT THE INFORMATION PROTECTION PLAYBOOK

The *Information Protection Playbook* was created from successful practices in global organizations, benchmarking, advice from a variety of subject-matter experts, and feedback from the organizations involved with the Security Executive Council. It is driven by business requirements, laws, and regulations, and provides an overall model for developing a comprehensive IP program.

The primary objective of IP is to provide the balance of adequate security at a reasonable cost. IP protects the interests of those relying on information, and protects the applications, systems, and networks that deliver the information from failures of:

- Confidentiality, which assures that information is observed by or disclosed to only those who have a need to know;
- Integrity, which assures that information is in its expected state, protected against unauthorized modification;
- Availability, which assures that information is available and usable when required and that the systems providing it can appropriately resist attacks and recover from failures;
- Trust and accountability, a requirement for electronic business transactions and information exchanges between customers; suppliers and partners; and
- Privacy, which assures that the organization will protect personally identifiable information (PII) entrusted to it by its customers, suppliers, and partners, as required by law and regulation.

The *Information Protection Playbook* identifies five major IP functions as the necessary and sufficient components of an IP framework, as shown in Figure A. These are driven by business objectives, laws, regulations, and industry standards. The IP functions span business processes, physical information assets, and information technology such as networking, systems, and applications, as well as data.

This playbook proposes that you engage in a holistic review of your IP program. This exercise is intended to give you and your higher

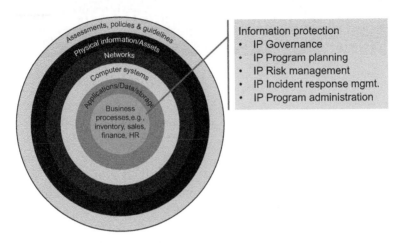

*Figure A **Information Protection Framework** These five functions are broken down further into a series of objectives or milestones to be achieved in order to implement the framework. It is an organizational decision which of the objectives are addressed first, but each of them must be attained in some manner.*

management a mechanism to assess what your IP program is doing and identify areas where improvements are necessary. This also offers a means to gain assurance that your processes are aligned with those of other leading organizations. Your organization may be already doing many or even most of the things that are described in the sections that follow. If your organization determines that you're fully aligned with the functions and objectives presented here, then the continued refinement of key planning functions and the improvement in your ability to execute the IP mission will offer rewarding opportunities for improvement. On the other hand, if your organization is not able to demonstrate alignment with the functions of the framework and cannot meet the proposed objectives of the playbook, you will want to concentrate your energies and investments on the IP fundamentals not being accomplished as revealed by this process. This would allow them to organize improvements to IP planning and execution in a coherent, planned approach.

Please be aware, this playbook is not a resource for the detailed subject matter required to enable an organization to deploy a fully function information protection plan. Rather, like the playbooks used in team sports, it describes in a brief form what takes professionals years to learn. Like professional athletes, it also requires an ongoing determination to learn new things and practice existing skills in order to master the field of information protection.

IP PROGRAM

An effective IP program will include the following five functions. This program is based on a model promoted by the Information Systems Audit and Control Association (ISACA) and validated by thousands of Certified Information Security Managers. These functions will be used as the means to explain the subordinate objectives of the *Information Protection Playbook* and each of them will be explored in more detail in the sections that follow.

1. Governance
2. Program Planning
3. Risk Management
4. Incident Response Management
5. Program Administration

INTRODUCTION

The global business economy continues to experience an increase in the complexity, scope, and cost of risk management and risk control from many and varied demands. These range from increasingly stringent security and privacy legislation, expanding industry standards, and continuing and emergent technical vulnerabilities. Given these issues, it is critical to build an information protection (IP) program within every global organization that is proactive; to identify the key risks and invest accordingly to mitigate those risks; and to avoid, at all cost, having an IP program that is threat-driven and reactive. As reported by Symantec:

- Symantec blocked a total of over 5.5 billion malware attacks in 2011, an 81 percent increase over 2010.
- Web-based attacks increased by 36 percent with over 4,500 new attacks each day.
- 403 million new variants of malware were created in 2011, a 41 percent increase of 2010.
- 39 percent of malware attacks via email used a link to a web page.
- Mobile vulnerabilities continued to rise, with 315 discovered in 2011.[1]

McAfee similarly reports:

- Android threats now reach almost 7,000, with more than 8,000 total mobile malware in their database.
- As of first quarter 2012, McAfee had collected more than 83 million samples in their combined "malware zoo."
- Despite global levels dropping, spear-phishing and spam are as dangerous as ever. Monthly averages of legitimate email messages (approximately 500 billion messages per month) are still significantly dwarfed by the number of spam messages (approximately 1.2 trillion messages per month).

---

[1]Symantec, "Internet Security Threat Report 2013."

- Global botnet infections reached approximately 4.5 million as of March 2012.[2]

It continues to be more difficult and consumes more resources to mount a continuous and global enterprise defense. The adversaries being encountered have undergone a significant shift from those days when hackers were intent on vandalism and focused on symbolic acts to claim credit for compromising a system. Where the adversaries of the past might have sought peer recognition for penetrating a system to deface a web page or plant a file to note the break-in, the current generations of attackers are predominantly highly skilled agents of governments or criminal organizations seeking the theft of money, valuable intellectual property, or other information assets.

The barriers continue to ease for attackers. Emergent (or zero-day) attacks can cover the world in less time than it takes to react. A recent example is the Zeus Trojan Horse, which is responsible for an estimated 3.6 million compromised systems between 2007 and 2013, resulting in compromises to credit data at more than 15 unnamed global banks and an estimated loss in excess of $70 million reported in the United States alone. Unreported losses are rumored to be much larger. Zeus has evolved from its origins as an email-based phishing exploit to now include attacks on mobile devices. It has mutated into family of malware variants since its code was leaked in 2011.[3]

To deal with current and future risk management complexity, organizations must:

- Design, develop, and deploy an IP strategic direction with objectives that align with business objectives.
- Design, develop, and deploy an IP framework, such as the one presented in this playbook, to implement the IP strategic direction and objectives.
- Integrate IP risk management across business and corporate functions.

---

[2]McAfee Labs, "McAfee Threats Report."
[3]Information about the Zeus Trojan Horse was obtained from a variety of publicly available sources, including Symantec (www.symantec.com), Krebs on Security (https://krebsonsecurity.com/), and SC Magazine (http://www.scmagazine.com/).

• Socialize the IP program throughout the organization using awareness and training programs to motivate employees, contractors, vendors, suppliers, and other key stakeholders.

ASSUMPTIONS

The creation of an effective IP program requires a holistic approach that encompasses all of the elements identified in this playbook. Without effective execution of each of these elements, it is not likely that an organization will be able to form an effective IP framework. It is assumed that any organization seeking to deliver IP capabilities will have:

1. An IP strategic review process is integral to ongoing operations. This requires four specific areas of focus: policies, roles and responsibilities, security awareness, and the output from the completion of a self-assessment checklist.
2. An IP governance framework that has implemented basic governance processes and includes periodic review to pursue continuous improvement to align IP governance structures with organizational goals and objectives.
3. An enterprise-wide risk management program.

IP STRATEGY

In order to integrate into business processes, it is critical that IP be aligned with the company's key business strategies. To achieve

Figure B IP adds value by enabling the business to achieve its goals.

alignment, IP needs to understand the business strategies and business objectives. Policies that support the business strategies and objectives must then be developed. Once the first two steps are completed, the IP framework can be defined and implemented. To achieve the desired result, executive management must buy into and support the plan. Figure B illustrates how a business process architecture builds on a process to assure business strategy alignment that should drive policy processes that will support a complete IP program framework.

CHAPTER 1

Information Protection Function One: Governance

The governance function establishes and maintains a framework to provide assurance that information protection strategies are aligned with business objectives and consistent with applicable laws and regulations. The objectives of the governance function and how they might best be implemented are as follows:

Objective	Implementation
1. Develop the IP strategy in support of business strategy and direction.	Strategic management
2. Obtain senior management commitment and support.	Reporting and communication
3. Ensure the definition and implementation of roles and responsibilities throughout the organization.	Roles and responsibilities
4. Establish reporting and communication channels that support IP governance activities.	Reporting and communication
5. Identify and assess the impact of current and potential legal and regulatory issues.	Regulations and compliance management
6. Establish and maintain policies that support business goals and objectives.	Policies
7. Ensure the development of procedures and guidelines that support the policies.	Procedures and guidelines
8. Develop business case and organization value analysis that support IP program investments.	Portfolio management

IP is fundamentally a management problem, and its effectiveness is significantly impacted by the organization's approach to governance. The implementation of sound IP will require the following seven governance-related implementations.

IMPLEMENTATION ONE: STRATEGIC MANAGEMENT

Strategic management is the process of making and implementing strategic decisions. It is a mechanism used to bring change to organizations to facilitate the movement from what the organization is toward what the

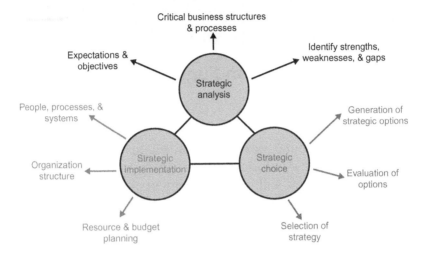

Figure 1.1 Strategic Management.

organization seeks to become. Creating an IP strategy requires that the organization knows and understands its current resources and capabilities for IP functionality, and also knows and understands the threats that are present in the operational environment. The potential for a value-adding strategy lies in management's ability to identify opportunity for managed change, and to move toward the desired future state with the resources available for such a change. Strategy is the vehicle that uses an organization's objectives to design, develop, and deploy policies that will guide its activities as it moves to achieve its desired future state. As shown in Figure 1.1, there are three main elements of strategic management in this context:

1. Strategic analysis: Understanding an organization's strategic situation
2. Strategic choice: Choosing between courses of action
3. Strategic implementation: Putting the chosen course of action into effect

Major Milestones

Using this model of strategic management, the process can be resolved into six major milestones. Each of these milestones maps to one of the main elements.

	Milestones	Strategic Management Element
1.	Start-up	Strategic analysis
2.	Examine existing strategy	Strategic analysis
3.	Compare best practice	Strategic analysis
4.	Strategic options	Strategic choice
5.	Strategy and road map*	Strategic implementation
6.	Close-down*	Strategic implementation

Strategy and road map and close-down partly map onto the strategic implementation element of the model. The mapping is partial as the actual roll-out of the implementation of the strategy occurs over several years.

Six Strategic Management Milestones

1. Start-up

During the start-up part of the process, there is agreement on the details of the work plan. The key deliverables from this part of the work are an agreed scope, plan, and schedule. Key aspects are:

- Create a preliminary definition of the Information Protection Management Group (called the IPM Group hereafter). Who is in the group, how does it operate, and who is the champion representing senior management.
- Agreeing on the scope of the work (i.e., what's in and what's out)— consider various dimensions: the locations, functions, and departments to cover.
- Brainstorming (and possibly using other creative management techniques) and agreeing to an initial set of key issues to address as part of the work.
- Agreeing to the plan—consider timeframes and milestones.
- Agreeing to the work schedule. Consider the candidates to interview (top managers and other key people) and the timescales, and draft a briefing note to give to relevant individuals.

2. Examine Existing Strategy

When examining existing strategy, a brief report on opinions, observations, comments, and key issues will be completed. The following tasks will be done:

- Understand the business drivers for IP as the motivation for strategies within the organization.

- It is assumed that the members of the project team who are engaged in this process are familiar with the:
  - Statement of the organization's values (sometimes referred to as an organization's operating principles). This might best be described as "the essential nature of the organization's culture."
  - Statement of the organization's vision. This might best be described as "where the organization is headed."
  - Statement of the organization's mission (often referred to as a mission statement). This might best be described as "how will the organization get to where it is headed."

  Many organizations use these core documents to prepare an annual list of strategic objectives.

- Conduct interviews with the organization's top-level managers and other key people to solicit their insights, views, comments, and ideas concerning IP in the organization. The following areas will be explored:
  - What (realistic) position does the organization currently give to IP?
  - What are the main threats to the organization's business over the next three years?
  - How is risk management effected and what is the organization's appetite for risk?
  - What is the organization's attitude toward enforcement of IP polices (soft—with incentives, hard—with sanctions, mix of soft and hard—in what proportions)?
  - Budget provision for IP—historic/current/currently anticipated for the future?
- Study the IP department to understand the department's:
  - Structure and organization (especially how it relates to other areas of the organization).
  - Objectives and targets (i.e., what are its current drivers?).
  - Processes and functions (i.e., what is actually done and achieved?).

3. Compare Best Practice

When comparing best practice, a report on strengths, weaknesses, and gaps will be completed. The following tasks will be done:

- Gather relevant information from various regulations and guidelines, and draw upon relevant experience with other companies. Possible sources of relevant information are:
  - Sarbanes-Oxley Act (United States), European Union's Data Protection Directive, Canada's PIPEDA, OECD's Guidelines on

the Protection of Privacy, FTC Fair Information Practices, HIPAA, HITECH, GLBA, Safe Harbor, and so on.
- ISO 27000 series, NIST, COBIT, NFPA 1600, British Standards Institution (BSI), PAS 56:2003 (Guide to Business Continuity Management).

• Undertake the best practice comparison, identifying the strengths and weaknesses of the organization's existing IP organization, practices, and operations as well as the threats and opportunities the organization faces at the present time. Some organizations call this process and the resulting assessment a SWOT analysis.
• Identify and assess any gaps. This would highlight any missing practices, misaligned objectives, and inefficiencies (particular attention will be paid to any areas where potential cost savings could be made and/or critical investment is needed).

4. Strategic Options

During the strategic options part of the process, a report on the strategic options and their change implications will be provided. There is a need to consider "strategic fit" of the options; for example, is the proposed strategy suitable, feasible, and acceptable to the organization? Is it playing to key strengths, exploiting opportunities, capitalizing on distinctive competencies? Will it meet the organization's objectives? Will it fit the organization's management values and culture? Will it be acceptable to the organization's stakeholders? The following tasks, which will require working very closely with key organization staff, will be done:

• Develop and discuss strategic options for the future of IP within the organization. These options may cover such areas as: organization, relationships, processes, standards, skills, resources, technologies, and knowledge base.
• Consider the implications of these options for strategic change within the organization. Explore positive drivers and negative resistance factors for the strategic change.
• Prepare and give a presentation to key people in the organization.
• In coordination with the organization, select the most appropriate strategic options to take forward.

5. Strategy and Road Map

During the strategy and road map part of the process, a documented IP strategy and a road map for its implementation over the next several years will be provided. The following tasks, which will require working very closely with key organization staff, will be done:

- Develop and document the IP strategy for the organization.
- Develop a road map for the next two to three years. This will be a high-level implementation plan for the rollout of the IP strategy for the organization. This document will deal with priorities and time-frames for the various components of the IP strategy. Draft, first-cut budgets, and resource levels will also be proposed wherever possible.
- Prepare and give a presentation to communicate the strategy and road map to key members of the organization.

6. Close-Down
During the close-down part of the process, a brief report will be provided on the lessons learned. The key aspect to include in the report is:

- Reflecting on the work and documenting what went well and any areas of future improvement.

Key Points of the Strategic Management Process
As the governance management process proceeds, keep in mind eight crucial issues that should be addressed:

1. Assure the alignment of IP strategy with the organization's business objectives.
2. Verify that the organization's risk appetite is well understood, and that it accurately reflects management's attitude toward the risk of operating and information systems.
3. Confirm that IP activities are well coordinated with and mutually supportive of business processes.
4. Document the implemented approach to IP investment.
5. Finalize the structure, organization, and placement of the IP group.
6. Define the future structure of the IP group, identify resources that will be needed for those plans, and define the future state skills mix.
7. Plan for the integration and assimilation of IP strategy throughout the organization.
8. Have a defined plan for sustaining the IP strategy.

IMPLEMENTATION TWO: REPORTING AND COMMUNICATION

Visibility of IP program structures and processes is important. Many organizations have an unstated posture of maintaining a low visibility for IP actions among outside stakeholders, and some organizations will also downplay IP elements within the organization. In the current environment, IP structures and actions should be promoted to all stakeholders inside and outside of the organization. An effective communications strategy for IP initiatives will accrue improved effectiveness for the IP program. The attitude that risk management and security functions should be silent and hidden is incorrect. There should be a defined communication process so that critical information regarding IP actions and events can be reliable and regularly transmitted to executive management, specifically the chief executive officer (CEO), as well as tailoring messages to all stakeholders as appropriate.

For example, as initiatives are undertaken to meet regulatory compliance requirements or as part of a periodic refresh effort, internal reporting channels should be used to make announcements of progress.

- For instance, report when disaster recovery plans are prepared or revised.
- Whenever a business disruption involves the activation of the disaster plan, status reports on the recovery operation, up to and including final resolution, should be made internally available to the organization. External communications on the matter should occur after full resumption of normal business operations.
- Perhaps, if privacy policy or practices regarding handling of personal information are being revised, relevant announcements can be made.
- When external validations of IP practices are received, these should also be reported internally, and perhaps externally. For example, when a Sarbanes-Oxley periodic audit comes in with a positive result, this could generate positive reporting in internal reporting channels. Major milestones and completion of significant projects should also be reported in this way.

One essential aspect of the communication strategy is to deliver frequent executive and board-level briefings on IP status and issues. These presentations should use suitable abstract and high-level perspectives to provide the overall context of IP in the organization. Appendix B has a sample presentation.

IMPLEMENTATION THREE: POLICIES

In general, IP policies will state that physical and digital business-critical information systems must be protected; set the rules for expected behavior by all employees, nonemployees, and management; and describe the consequences of noncompliance. IP policies assert that information is an asset, is the property of the organization, and is to be protected from unauthorized access, modification, disclosure, and destruction.

A benchmark study of policies representing a cross-section of industries was conducted by the Security Executive Council. This included high revenue/global companies, government organizations, universities, and institutions (see Acknowledgments section). Commonly cited examples were identified and are listed.

Key Points
1. The security executive most often has an advisory role, not an enforcement role.
2. There should be consequences for noncompliance of policy.
3. Sign-off procedures and new hire programs are in place.
4. All elements of a holistic communication strategy, and especially the security awareness program for employees, must be directly tied to organizational policies.
5. One critical policy, often neglected, is a data classification policy. This enables the organization to devote proportional efforts to protecting critical data. An example of certain aspects of such a policy is included in a list of recommended policies found in Appendix C.

IMPLEMENTATION FOUR: REGULATIONS AND COMPLIANCE MANAGEMENT

Compliance with global IP security and privacy regulations is a daunting task for most chief security officers (CSO) and chief information security officers (CISO). As a starting point, a global cross-functional team composed of Human Resources (HR), Information Technology (IT), Security, Audit, Marketing, Legal, Finance, and others as needed, needs to be assembled to determine which regulations impact the organization. Tools that help deal with the complexity of managing multiple regulations, standards, and guidelines, such as the Security Executive Council's

RoCM (Regulation and Compliance Management) application, can be very beneficial.[1]

IMPLEMENTATION FIVE: ROLES AND RESPONSIBILITIES

In most settings, it's recommended that the corporate security executive is the facilitator of the IP program. A strategic global IP steering committee (GIPSC) should be implemented to provide executive-level governance and direction. The GIPSC should be composed of representatives from key business units: IT, HR, Finance, Legal, Audit, Business Continuity, Risk Management, Marketing, and Corporate Security.

Various tactical governance bodies should be also implemented, composed of management-level representatives from the business unit owners (applications, divisional infrastructure, and remote sites), enterprise application owners (e.g., HR, Finance, and Procurement), technology area owners (e.g., Enterprise Networks, Platforms, and Help Desk), and from Enterprise Information Security and Internal Audit. These groups are empowered to focus on day-to-day security, privacy, disaster recovery planning (DRP) execution, and operations for infrastructure and applications.

Many organizations find that the development of a Responsibility, Accountability, Consult, and Inform (RACI) matrix can add significant value to the IP program and increase cross-departmental coordination. An example of a representative RACI has been provided in Appendix D and was culled from available documentation from exemplary companies (see Acknowledgments section for additional source information). In addition, experts representing several companies were consulted in the preparation of the information on position titles and position descriptions.

Key Points

1. The security executive is seen as a facilitator. Higher management must function as an arbiter among competing management perspectives, seeking to balance these competing interests for the best outcome for the whole of the organization. The information security working groups (e.g., system/application administrators, disaster recovery planners) operate as the implementers of controls (of which the security

---

[1]For more information about the Security Executive Council's Regulation and Compliance Management Tool, visit: https://www.securityexecutivecouncil.com/common/streamfile.html? PROD = 164&cti = 24904.

executive manages). The auditing groups serve the vital role of enforcing policy and assuring that members of the organization conform to the will of senior management as expressed in that policy.

2. Roles and responsibilities must be carefully defined, fully documented, and clearly communicated to those that have roles identified in the RACI.

Figure 1.2 illustrates how an organization might structure and communicate the roles and responsibilities by seeking consensus from stakeholders and identifying target audiences for communication efforts. A detailed example of a representative RACI roles and responsibilities matrix is provided in Appendix D. Additional information about position titles and position descriptions is provided in Appendix J.

IMPLEMENTATION SIX: PROCEDURES AND GUIDELINES

A process needs to be in place to ensure the timely addition and/or modification of IP procedures. Examples of these procedures include:

- Granting access to consumers, when requested, to view or change their personal information.
- Providing business continuity plan templates to the business units.
- Controlling access to critical sites.

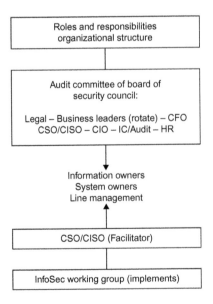

Figure 1.2 Roles and Responsibilities in the Organization.

IMPLEMENTATION SEVEN: PORTFOLIO MANAGEMENT

It is very important to integrate with the portfolio/project management office for two primary reasons:

1. To ensure that all IP projects are cost justified and to get an enterprise view of IP expenditures.
2. To ensure that all the organization's projects (assuming they are in the portfolio) will trigger an IP review.

GOVERNANCE IMPROVEMENT

Every functioning organization has a method of governance in place, even if the method is unplanned and unimproved. All organizations, even the biggest and best, must look for the means to make continuous improvements in the approach used to provide the necessary governance structure and managerial oversight to IP processes.

One aspect to consider for this ongoing review is to look for opportunities to leverage convergence of the various IP processes and organizational units involved in IP. When possible, the convergence of existing processes should be examined for the opportunity to reduce costs and/or to improve service delivery.

ADDITIONAL INFORMATION

The following resources are recommended as reputable sources of additional guidance for governance improvement activities:

- IT Governance Institute, *Board Briefing on IT Governance*, 2nd edition, 2003. http://www.isaca.org/restricted/Documents/26904_Board_Briefing_final.pdf.
- IT Governance Institute, *Information Security Governance: Guidance for Boards of Directors and Executive Management*, 2nd edition, 2006. http://www.isaca.org/Knowledge-Center/Research/Documents/InfoSecGuidanceDirectorsExecMgt.pdf.
- IT Governance Institute, *Information Security Governance: Guidance for Information Security Managers*, 2008. http://www.isaca.org/Knowledge-Center/Research/ResearchDeliverables/Pages/Information-Security-Governance-Guidance-for-Information-Security-Managers.aspx.

CHAPTER 2

Information Protection Function Two: Program Planning

This function designs, develops, and structures an IP program to implement an IP governance model as developed from the process recommended in Information Protection Function One: Governance.

The objectives and key elements of the IP program planning function are listed in the following table. Each key element will be subsequently discussed in greater detail. The baselines key element and the key element of standards, procedures, and guidelines will be grouped into one section below; similarly, the accountability and resources elements will also be discussed in one section.

Objective	Key Element
1. Create and maintain plans to implement the IP governance framework.	Plans
2. Develop IP baselines.	Baselines
3. Develop procedures and guidelines to ensure business processes address IP risk.	Standards, procedures, and guidelines
4. Develop standards, procedures, and guidelines for IP infrastructure activities to ensure compliance with IP policies.	Standards, procedures, and guidelines
5. Integrate IP program requirements into the organization's life cycle activities.	Standards, procedures, and guidelines
6. Develop methods of meeting IP policy requirements that recognize impact on end-users.	Standards, procedures, and guidelines
7. Promote accountability by business process owners and other stakeholders in managing IP security risks.	Accountability
8. Establish metrics to manage the IP governance framework.	Metrics
9. Ensure that internal and external resources for IP are identified, appropriated, and managed.	Resources

BASELINES, STANDARDS, PROCEDURES, AND GUIDELINES

Included in this area are the baseline IP services, which are imbedded within the business processes to address risk.

The following baseline services are to be provided by the IP group and other key services providers:

- Policies, standards, guidelines, and procedures
- IP risk assessments for technologies/architecture and applications
- Disaster recovery planning (DRP)
- Security awareness, education, and training
- Security architecture development and management (e.g., virus, firewall, intrusion detection system, etc.)
- Vulnerability assessment
- Security and access administration
- Enterprise incident response (see Information Protection Function Four: Incident Response Management section)
- Self-assessment checklist (see Appendix G)

ACCOUNTABILITY AND RESOURCES

Accountability is addressed via the roles and responsibilities matrix in Appendix D.

In summary:

- The global security steering committee will set overall direction and goals and approve information security policies and initiatives.
- Depending on the governance choices made by senior management, the CISO or CIO will have overall accountability for the information security, privacy, and DRP functions.
- The vice president(s) have overall accountability for ensuring IP controls are implemented for the business critical information in their areas of responsibility.
- Divisional managers, technology area owners, and business application owners are accountable for security administration, initial information risk assessment, and maintenance of IP standards for their information, applications, and infrastructure.
- The enterprise IP group is accountable for:
  - Information security, privacy, and DRP policies and standards.
  - Ensuring compliance with information security, privacy, and disaster recovery legislation.
  - Information security, privacy, and DRP risk identification and reporting.
  - Enterprise incident monitoring and response coordination.
  - Coordinating ongoing information security, privacy, and DRP audits.

- Information security, privacy, and DRP awareness, training, and education.
• The internal audit group is accountable for performing periodic independent audits of the controls environment and compliance with laws, regulations, and policies.
• The external auditor is accountable for external audits.
• Corporate security is accountable for physical security and controls, and often owns the relationships with external law enforcement agencies and runs investigations.
• HR is responsible for accurate and timely information on employee status and reporting lines to enable access processes for approval (management structure) and timely removal (leavers).
• Procurement is responsible for proper vendor and contractor management to ensure information for timely access processes for contractors (this includes not only enabling access when needed but also the timely deactivation of access when it is no longer required), and vendor/contractor acceptance of compliance to internal security policies.
• The labor relations group is responsible for ensuring employee investigation procedures are handled properly and that consequences to policy violations are applied consistently and appropriately.

METRICS

Metrics, also known as performance measurement, provides a means to assess performance by measuring specific outcomes and providing comparison to prior measurements (baselines); comparison to intended results (trends); or comparison against outside references (benchmarks). After an initial cycle of collection, organizations can assess some aspects of the security profile by comparing relevant measures against the internal baseline from an earlier measurements baseline.

The following metrics should be considered for implementation by many organizations:

• Comparison to baseline standards
  - "Top ##" items for network, platform, and application layers
• Trend analysis
  - Month-to-month trending
  - Measured versus objective
• Comparison to external benchmarks

- Comparison to compliance frameworks (ISO 27000, PCI security standards, etc.)
- Program or operational effectiveness
  - Summary reporting of incidents (virus or vulnerability exploits) within the network
  - Numbers of probes or scans that penetrated the network
  - Counts of specific, well-known, or high-visibility attacks
  - Overall effectiveness score: Systems availability compared to outages and mitigation effort/cost above the baseline
  - Measurements on IT maintenance processes, such as time to patch and the percentage of systems at current patch levels, or the number of machines without functioning antivirus
  - Measurements on time to grant or revoke access
  - Number of systems that meet policy standards
  - Number of open risks in risk register not mitigated within service level agreements (SLAs)
  - Percentage of systems/networks/etc. that meet regulatory requirements
- Effectiveness of projects for specific risk mitigation initiatives
  - Comparison of current status to baseline before the project began
  - Progress relative to end goals
- Financial
  - Operational financial performance for routine activities
  - Project and incident financial performance for projects and incident response operations
  - Annual benchmark of organization vs. "like industry" competitors

For additional information on IT and information security metrics, see Appendix K as well as NIST Special Publication 800-55, Rev. 1, "Performance Measurement Guide for Information Security," http://csrc.nist.gov/publications/nistpubs/800-55-Rev1/SP800-55-rev1.pdf.

FOR MORE INFORMATION

The Security Executive Council has a comprehensive text that contains descriptions of hundreds of proven measures, including many in the area of information protection. It is titled *Measures and Metrics in Corporate Security: Communicating Business Value* by George K. Campbell. A new edition of this title will be available from Elsevier in 2014.

CHAPTER 3

Information Protection Function Three: Risk Management

To achieve business objectives, the IP team should identify and manage information security risks. The objectives and key elements of the risk management function are as follows. Each key element is subsequently discussed in greater detail.

Objective	Key Element
1. Develop a systematic, analytical, and continuous risk management process.	Risk assessment
2. Ensure that risk identification, analysis, and mitigation activities are integrated into lifecycle processes.	Risk assessment
3. Apply risk identification and analysis methods.	Risk assessment
4. Define strategies and prioritize options to mitigate risk to levels acceptable to the enterprise.	Risk prioritization procedure
5. Report significant changes in risk to appropriate levels of management on both a periodic and event-driven basis.	Risk communication procedure

RISK ASSESSMENT

At a high level, there are threats that exploit vulnerabilities in the IT infrastructure. The combination of the threat/vulnerability pairs then create consequences to the business, as illustrated in Figure 3.1.

Risk Assessment Procedure

A risk assessment framework should be implemented to analyze risks. Below is an example:

RISK =

PROBABILITY   X   IMPACT

[Threats x
(Vulnerabilities –
Countermeasures)]   Business Consequences

Assessed by IP Group   Assessed by Business

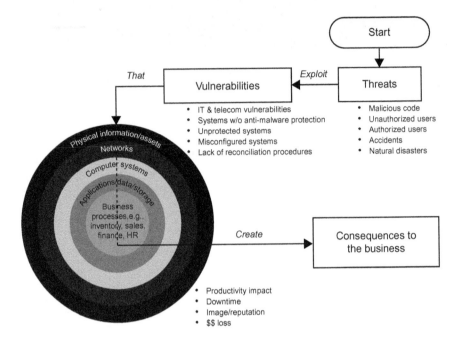

Figure 3.1 Finding Risk.

Threats are classified as external (e.g., hackers, worms, viruses), internal (e.g., employees, contractors), and natural (e.g., hurricanes, tornadoes, floods, lightning, fire).

The internal service providers (e.g., IT security, network services, developers, infrastructure/system administrators, help desk, etc.) need to have a mastery of the tools necessary to identify vulnerabilities. These tools enable skilled staff to identify and verify vulnerabilities, including those from operating systems caused by failures to maintain patching levels or deficiencies in configuration, along with vulnerabilities from layered products (such as databases, web servers, or middleware) and deficiencies in commonly encountered applications. These staff should also be experts at using manual self-assessment tools to determine specific application security gaps.

The business unit, with guidance and leadership by the IP group, determines the consequences to the business.

The vulnerabilities and threats that lead to significant impact to the business are mitigated via the implementation of the appropriate countermeasures.

Risk Prioritization Procedure

Once the risks are identified using the risk assessment procedure, the risks should be mapped into a risk prioritization mechanism. A sample of such a mechanism is shown in Figure 3.2. In the "red area" are the high impact and high probability risks that must be addressed first.

Key Points

1. It is of fundamental importance to prioritize risks (or the aggregate of a category of risks) at the enterprise level and align relevance to other business risks. This will allow the appropriate resources to be allocated in mitigating those risks that are deemed highest priority to a particular organization.[1]
2. A designated IP council should approve the priorities, projects, and resources needed to mitigate risk. It is understood that certain organizations have other processes (e.g., portfolio management) that approve projects; in this case there has to be coordination among the processes.

RISK COMMUNICATION PROCEDURE

Using representative examples, this procedure is shown in Figure 3.2. This process can be combined with the reporting and communication procedure from Information Protection Function One: Governance to enable resilience across the organization.

RISK MANAGEMENT METHODOLOGIES

There are a number of popular methodologies and sources of guidance available to support an effective risk management program, including:

- OCTAVE (www.cert.org/octave)
- ISO 27005 standard for information security risk management http://www.27000.org/iso-27005.htm
- National Institute of Standards and Technology (NIST) Computer Security Resource Center: http://csrc.nist.gov/publications/PubsSPs.html
  - Managing Information Security Risk: Organization, Mission, and Information System View (SP 800-39)

---

[1]There is an example matrix of risks prioritized by **High**, **Medium**, and **Low** levels in Appendix E.

Impact (business consequences)			
High	Due to attacks, an organization's websites are not available for use and/or data is compromised, leading to image and customer service issues.	Data could be released or compromised, leading to customer, partner, or employee liability as well as a negative impact to image.	Data and IT infrastructure for critical business processes run in the DMZ are compromised by attackers or malware, leading to loss of availability with impacts to productivity and a negative impact to image.
Medium	Inadequate change control procedures cause unexpected application downtime, making critical business systems temporarily unavailable.	Improperly validated changes to firewall rules result in employee access to Web locations prohibited by policy leading to potentially creating a hostile workplace.	Improperly trained employees victimized by social engineering attack reveal sensitive data to attacker, leading to customer, partner, or employee liability as well as a negative impact to image.
Low	Unexpected action by software consultant changes application behavior, resulting in inaccurate application performance.	Unexpected power outage reveals flaws in data center power backup plans and systems sustain temporary unplanned outage.	Internal systems unavailable due to employee triggering of malware on client computer.
	Low	**Medium**	**High**
	Probability of loss (Likelihood of a loss from a threat based on the existence of vulnerabilities and considering the controls currenty in place)		

Figure 3.2 Information Security Threats—Countermeasure Focus Areas.

- Guide for Applying the Risk Management Framework to Federal Information Systems: A Security Life Cycle Approach (SP 800-37, Rev.1)
- Guide for Conducting Risk Assessments (SP 800-30, Rev 1)
- Microsoft's Security Risk Management Guide http://www.microsoft.com/en-us/download/details.aspx?id = 6232

Which methodology is chosen is less important than the decision to choose, implement, and enforce compliance to any methodology. Any effective risk management methodology will include three basic stages:

1. Risk Identification
2. Risk Assessment
3. Risk Control

Risk identification and assessment are discussed earlier in this chapter. Risk control is the determination of risk strategy based on a gap analysis of current protection methods to the level of risk resulting from the risk assessment. If there is a gap between the amount of protection currently provided for a particular information asset, the organization can choose to do one or a combination of the following:

1. Implement additional controls
2. Transfer the risk to a third party (such as insurance or a managed security organization)
3. Mitigate the effect of a successful attack with effective incident response procedures
4. Accept the current level of risk, as-is
5. Remove the asset from exposure, by retiring or discontinuing use of the asset

FOR MORE INFORMATION

The following resource is recommended as a reputable source of additional guidance for risk management improvement activities:

- National Institute of Standards and Technology (NIST), "Managing Information Security Risk: Organization, Mission, and Information System View," SP 800-39, March 2011. http://csrc.nist.gov/publications/nistpubs/800-39/SP800-39-final.pdf

CHAPTER 4

Information Protection Function Four: Incident Response Management

This function develops and manages a capability to respond to and recover from disruptive and destructive events. The objectives and key elements of the incident response management function are as follows. Each key element will be subsequently discussed in greater detail.

Objective	Key Element
1. Develop and implement processes for detecting, identifying, and analyzing security-related events.	Process
2. Develop response and recovery plans, including organizing, training, and equipping the teams.	Plans
3. Ensure periodic testing of the response and recovery plans where appropriate.	Exercises
4. Ensure the execution of response and recovery plans as required.	Activation
5. Establish procedures for documenting an event as a basis for subsequent action, including forensics, training, or potential legal actions when necessary.	Documentation
6. Manage post-event reviews to identify causes and corrective actions.	Improvement

PROCESS

An example of a process is the strategic deployment of intrusion detection systems sensors throughout the internal and external network. The policies and rules for these systems need to be managed by the IP group.

Another critical process is to subscribe to receive alerts of security incidents from mailing lists (e.g., BugTraq), early alerting vendors (e.g., Symantec), or antiviral vendors (e.g., Symantec, McAfee, or TrendMicro). Besides vendor alerting, there should be internal procedures which alert the IP group to possible incidents.

PLANS, EXERCISES, ACTIVATION, DOCUMENTATION, AND IMPROVEMENT

Business continuity and recovery plans should be developed, documented, and tested by the owners of critical business information. See Appendix H for an example.

Incident response plans for the enterprise, the sites, and the incident reporting center (IRC) should be documented by the responsible parties. Once an incident is identified, the incident response team (IRT) analyzes the incident and makes the declaration to the IRC and implements the appropriate incident response plan (IRP).

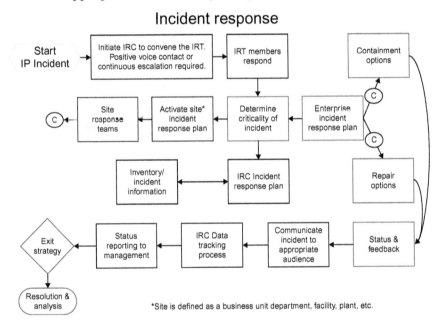

Figure 4.1 Incident Response.

There should be an enterprise-level IRP coordinated by the IP group which feeds from the divisional incident response plan (DIRP). In case of an incident, the IP group manages the event. On a quarterly basis, the communications portion of the IRP is activated to ensure the IRT members can be reached. Occasionally, mock exercises are conducted to provide training and to test, review, and update the plans.

Prior to exiting the IRP after it has been activated (for example, after a worm or virus has penetrated the internal systems), the networks are continuously scanned to ensure the threat has been eliminated. Depending on the type of incident, forensics procedures are invoked and executed (e.g., a disgruntled employee plants Trojans on certain systems). The last step of the IRP calls for a post-mortem to ensure lessons learned are discussed and enhancements to the plan implemented.

FOR MORE INFORMATION

The following resources are recommended as reputable sources of additional guidance for incident response improvement activities:

- National Institute of Standards and Technology (NIST), "Computer Security Incident Handling Guide," SP 800-61, Rev. 2, August 2012. http://csrc.nist.gov/publications/nistpubs/800-61rev2/SP800-61rev2.pdf
- Carnegie Mellon Software Engineering Institute, "Handbook for Computer Security Incident Response Teams (CSIRTs)," 2nd edition, April 2003. http://www.cert.org/archive/pdf/csirt-handbook.pdf

CHAPTER 5

Information Protection Function Five: Program Administration

This function organizes, manages, and conducts IP activities to execute the IP program. The objectives and key elements of the IP program administration function are as follows. Each key element will be subsequently discussed in greater detail (compliance-related elements are discussed as one topic below).

Objective	Key Element
1. Ensure that the use and protection of information complies with the enterprise's IP policies.	Internal compliance
2. Ensure that the administrative procedures for information systems comply with the enterprise's IP policies.	Internal compliance
3. Ensure that services provided by other enterprises, including outsourced providers, are consistent with established IP policies.	External (3rd party) compliance
4. Use metrics to measure, monitor, and report on the effectiveness of IP controls and compliance with IP security policies.	Metrics
5. Ensure that IP is not compromised throughout the change management process.	Change management
6. Ensure that vulnerability assessments are performed to evaluate the effectiveness of existing controls.	Internal compliance
7. Ensure that noncompliance issues and other variances are resolved in a timely manner.	Compliance
8. Ensure the development and delivery of the activities that can influence culture and behavior of staff, including IP security education and awareness.	Awareness

COMPLIANCE

A compliance measurement and reporting process should be in place to ensure compliance with policies and standards. (See Information Protection Function Two: Program Planning for a definition of the measurements that should be monitored.) For third-party services, contract terms and conditions should be implemented to address the IP requirements.

The IP group should meet regularly with the senior leadership (at least monthly) to address security, privacy, and disaster recovery issues and obtain commitment or timely implementation of security controls.

The global security steering committee will meet periodically (at least quarterly) to address policy issues.

Vulnerability assessments are to be performed for all reachable hosts that are in the network area that is public to the Internet, as well as hosts in any screened subnet with managed public access [commonly referred to as the demilitarized zone (DMZ)]. In addition, all mission-critical systems inside the network should be measured against baseline configuration and be fully assessed for vulnerabilities.

METRICS

The IP program administration function is the primary consumer of the metrics that are developed in IP program planning (see the Metrics section in Information Protection Function Two: Program Planning).

CHANGE MANAGEMENT

Change management practices, including configuration management to stabilize host system images and coordinated organization-wide change control practices, will be implemented. The efforts seek to assure maximum network and system reliability and uptime and minimize unscheduled downtime as an unintended consequence of unmanaged change.

Software Development and Deployment

Information security practices will be included in all systems development life cycle (SDLC) and change management processes adopted by the organization.

AWARENESS

The culture and behavior of the organization are to be addressed through ongoing security awareness education and training programs, such as monthly security "games" where all employees with email accounts can participate in answering questions related to policies and standards around security, privacy, and disaster recovery. Employees who do not have email accounts are targeted via other delivery mechanisms, such as posters and an annual computer security day.

An awareness program matrix has been developed based on standards and available documentation from exemplary companies (see the Acknowledgments). In addition, some aspects of the matrix are drawn from expert interviews and reflect the experiences of seasoned IP practitioners.

KEY POINTS

1. The security executive, as the advisor, will ensure that the protection of assets becomes the responsibility of the individual employees as identified in the RACI matrix.
2. Security awareness is critical because a security-unaware workforce becomes the weakest link in the chain.
3. A starting point to educate management and the workforce on IP policies and standards is the use of a self-assessment checklist (see Appendix G).
4. The easiest way to maintain and assess awareness is with regular exercises. They should be fun and rewarding. Provide instant feedback to the employee so he or she is aware of the correct answer.
5. For the training program, consider two metrics. First, track participation rates in training (often this is needed for compliance reasons, too). Second, consider doing an independent survey before starting a full training program, and then survey periodically for risky behaviors and knowledge. This can help track trends if the training is effective at changing behaviors.
6. Run periodic technology exercises (e.g., password cracking). Track performance trends over time and provide regular graphical feedback to departments. Often a cultivated sense of competition can lead to improved results.
7. The argument for a value proposition that encourages a security-aware culture should come from the highest levels of the organization, focused on headquarters or corporate and then drilled down into the individual business units.
8. Contractors and consultants are often a larger risk due to frequent turnover and poor intake procedures. These users will benefit from focused security awareness training above and beyond the policy acknowledgments that they sign.

FOR MORE INFORMATION

The following resources are recommended as reputable sources of additional guidance for information protection program administration:

- Michael Whitman and Herbert Mattord, *Management of Information Security*, 3rd ed. (Boston: Course Technology, 2010).
- National Institute of Standards and Technology (NIST), "Building an Information Technology Security Awareness and Training Program," SP800-50, October 2003. http://csrc.nist.gov/publications/nistpubs/800-50/NIST-SP800-50.pdf
- For security awareness and training matrix options, see Appendix F.
- Todd Fitzgerald and Micki Krause, eds., *CISO Leadership: Essential Principles for Success*, The (ISC)^2 Press Series (New York: Auerbach, 2007).
- Todd Fitzgerald, *Information Security Governance Simplified: From the Boardroom to the Keyboard* (Boca Raton: CRC Press, 2012).

Playbook Summary

WHAT'S HERE

This appendix provides an abridged version of the content in this playbook for ready reference.

HOW TO USE THIS APPENDIX

Use this synopsis as a quick reference to the items covered in the entire playbook.

SUMMARY

This playbook facilitates the development of a program to identify key risks and steer investment where they will most benefit the organization and offer the most IP as is possible within the limits of the available resources.

Your organization may be already doing many or even most of the things that are described in this summary. Please be aware that this playbook doesn't contain the detailed subject matter content necessary to enable an organization to deploy a fully functioning information protection plan. Rather, like the playbooks used in team sports, it describes in a brief, concise format what takes professionals years to learn. Like professional athletes, it also requires an ongoing determination to learn new things and practice existing skills in order to master the field of information protection.

The Security Executive Council has developed the *Information Protection Playbook* based on a framework composed of five major functions:

1. IP Governance
2. IP Program Planning

3. IP Risk Management
4. IP Incident Response Management
5. IP Program Administration

The order in which your organization pursues objectives is open to interpretation by your organization's management priorities, your organization's policies, and the relative priority established by the internal and external drivers of change within your organization. All must be addressed. Five core functions compose the critical functions of IP.

The **IP governance function** establishes and maintains a management template to provide assurance that information protection strategies are fully aligned with the objectives of your organization and are consistent with applicable laws and regulations. The principal objectives of the IP governance function are to:

1. Develop the IP strategy and direction in support of business strategy and direction. This is to assure alignment of IP strategy with business objectives.
2. Obtain senior management commitment and support. This is to assure sufficient management buy-in to achieve success.
3. Ensure the clear definition and full implementation of fully articulated roles and responsibilities throughout the organization. This is to eliminate ambiguity and make sure the correct staff are in place to meet IP objectives.
4. Establish reporting and communication channels that support IP governance activities.
5. Identify and assess the impact of current, emerging, and potential legal and regulatory issues.
6. Establish and maintain policies that support the goals and objectives of both IP and the overall business.
7. Ensure the development of standards, procedures, and guidelines that support those policies.
8. Develop business case and organization value analysis that supports IP program investments to assure that resources are well spent toward meeting stated objectives.

The **IP program planning function** designs, develops, and implements the IP program to institutionalize the IP governance framework.

The objectives and key elements of the IP program planning function are to:

1. Create and maintain plans to implement and maintain the IP governance framework.
2. Develop IP baselines.
3. Develop standards, procedures, and guidelines to ensure business processes address IP risk.
4. Develop standards, procedures, and guidelines for IP infrastructure activities to ensure compliance with IP policies.
5. Integrate IP program requirements into all the organization's life-cycle activities, especially those life-cycle methodologies implemented in information technology units of the organization.
6. Develop methods of meeting IP policy requirements that are sensitive of end-user impacts and that seek to provide a realistic balance of the need for functionality and the need for risk reduction.
7. Achieve accountability by business process owners and other stakeholders in managing IP security risks.
8. Establish measurement programs to identify, collect, and assess data (metrics) and use it in repeatable processes to manage the IP governance framework.
9. Ensure that those resources necessary to accomplish IP, both internal and external to the organization, are identified, funded, acquired, and managed.

The **IP risk management function** identifies and manages information protection risks to achieve business objectives. The principal objectives of the IP risk management function are to:

1. Develop a systematic, analytical, and continuous risk management process.
2. Ensure that risk identification, analysis, and mitigation activities are integrated into all life-cycle processes across the organization.
3. Apply risk identification and analysis methods consistently and uniformly throughout the organization.
4. Define strategies and prioritize options to mitigate risk to the levels that are acceptable to the enterprise, and ensure that those determining risk acceptance are making fully informed decisions about that risk.

5. Devise mechanisms that report all significant changes in risk to appropriate levels of management on both a periodic and event-driven basis.

The **IP incident response management function** develops and manages a capability to respond to and recover from disruptive and destructive events. The objectives and key elements of the IP incident response function are to:

1. Develop and implement processes for detecting, identifying, and analyzing IP-related events.
2. Develop response and recovery plans including organizing, training, and equipping the teams.
3. Ensure periodic testing of the response and recovery plans where appropriate.
4. Ensure the execution of response and recovery plans as required.
5. Establish procedures for documenting an event as a basis for subsequent action, including forensics when necessary.
6. Manage post-event reviews to identify causes and corrective actions.

The **IP program administration function** oversees and directs all IP activities to execute the IP program. The objectives and key elements of the IP program administration function are to:

1. Ensure that the standards, procedures, and guidelines for the use of information comply with the enterprise's IP policies.
2. Verify that the standards, procedures, and guidelines for the administration and operation of information systems comply with the enterprise's IP policies.
3. Ensure that services provided by other enterprises, including outsourced providers, are consistent with established IP policies.
4. Establish measurement programs to identify, collect, and assess data (metrics) and use it in repeatable processes to measure, monitor, manage, and report on the effectiveness of IP controls and overall compliance with IP policies.
5. Devise change management and change control standards, procedures, and guidelines to gain assurance that IP is not compromised by unmanaged change.
6. Establish programs of vulnerability assessment that continuously evaluate effectiveness of the existing IP control environment.

7. Devise standards, procedures, and guidelines to acquire and maintain compliance with regulatory and industry standards (for example, HIPAA, PCI DSS, and Sarbanes-Oxley, among others).[1] In addition, establish standards, procedures, and guidelines to resolve non-compliance issues and other variances with such regulatory and industry standards in a timely manner.
8. Influence your organization's culture and the behavior of staff through the development and delivery of an aggressive and engaging IP security education, training, and awareness program.

A number of tools, techniques, and templates are provided in the remaining appendices of this playbook.

---

[1] For more information about these example standards, visit http://www.hhs.gov/ocr/privacy/ for HIPAA, https://www.pcisecuritystandards.org/security_standards/ for the PCI Data Security Standard (PCI DSS), and http://www.sec.gov/spotlight/sarbanes-oxley.htm for the Sarbanes-Oxley Act of 2002.

Board of Directors Presentation

WHAT'S HERE

This appendix offers an example of a presentation that would be given to a board of directors. It identifies the type of information that might be included in such a presentation, and also shows how this information might best be communicated to executives at this level.

HOW TO USE THIS APPENDIX

Use this example to build your own presentation materials, which will communicate the value of IP to your senior-most executives and oversight authorities, such as directors, commissioners, and/or regulators.

EXAMPLE PRESENTATION

INFORMATION Protection Program

Information Protection (IP) Briefing
Board of Directors Presentation

Information Protection (IP) Briefing

Board of Directors
Audit Committee
Date:

Objective of IP

- Ensure the demonstrable confidentiality, integrity, and availability of the organization's information assets for authorized internal and external users by making our systems and applications secure from physical and cyber threat.

Strategy

- Layered protection against cyber-intrusion through internal and external controls. Physical controls against damage from physical threat; disaster recovery capability in case of need
- Documented processes, supported by systems to achieve and maintain compliance based on best practices and Sarbanes-Oxley disciplines
- Internal and external third-party verification
- Global IP Steering Committee as governance and oversight body

Audit Items

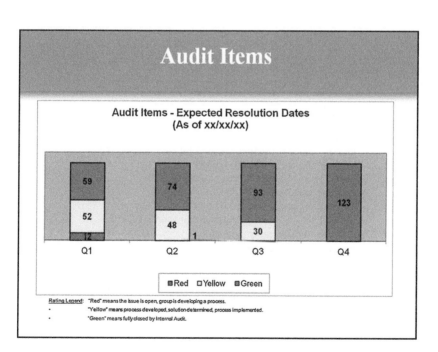

Audit Items - Expected Resolution Dates
(As of xx/xx/xx)

■Red   □Yellow   ■Green

Rating Legend: "Red" means the issue is open, group is developing a process.
·   "Yellow" means process developed, solution determined, process implemented.
·   "Green" means fully closed by Internal Audit.

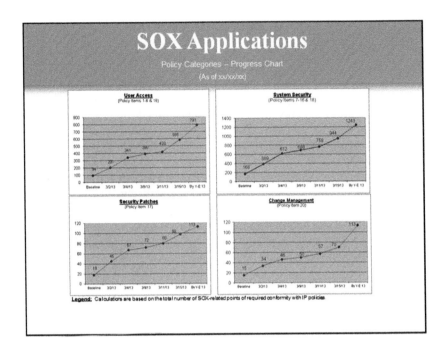

Current Status – 20xx IP Initiatives

(previous year)

- Develop security vision and enhance strategy
  - Validated the IT Security strategy and strengthened the governance mechanism
  - Reviewed policy & standards against global companies and ISO standards—no major deficiencies found
- Verify that audit points have been properly addressed
  - Significant recent progress
  - Supplemented management focus; initiated enhanced reporting
  - Global IP Steering Committee provides governance body
- Develop security awareness program
  - Program developed in 20xx
  - Awareness week xx/xx/xx
    - "xxxx" —branded logo for 20xx; brand characters delivering messages; local ambassadors; emphasis on role of individual employee in protecting information and facilities

Current Status – 20xx IP Initiatives
(current year)

- Disaster Recovery Planning
  - Plan and DR exercise completed. First test of multiple cross-divisional systems, involving approximately 50 applications, 100 different servers, 200 people, and one isolated network
  - Upgrades and increased coverage planned in 20xx for SOX-related applications
- Determine impact of Sarbanes-Oxley on IT information security
  - Developed strategy and action plans in four focus areas:
    - User Access
    - System Security
    - Security Patches
    - Change Management
  - Enhanced reporting of privileged accounts for cleanup and restriction
  - Inventoried systems requiring documentation of control

IP Strategy

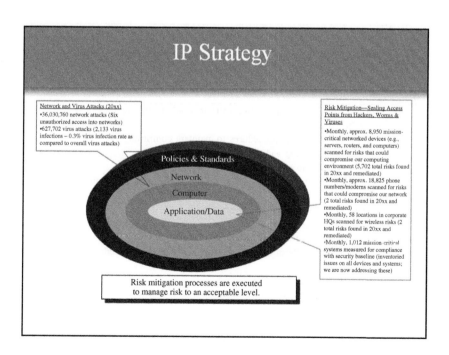

Network and Virus Attacks (20xx)
- 36,030,760 network attacks (Six unauthorized access into networks)
- 627,702 virus attacks (2,133 virus infections – 0.3% virus infection rate as compared to overall virus attacks)

Policies & Standards
Network
Computer
Application/Data

Risk Mitigation—Sealing Access Points from Hackers, Worms & Viruses
- Monthly, approx. 8,950 mission-critical networked devices (e.g., servers, routers, and computers) scanned for risks that could compromise our computing environment (5,702 total risks found in 20xx and remediated)
- Monthly, approx. 18,825 phone numbers/modems scanned for risks that could compromise our network (2 total risks found in 20xx and remediated)
- Monthly, 58 locations in corporate HQs scanned for wireless risks (2 total risks found in 20xx and remediated)
- Monthly, 1,012 mission-critical systems measured for compliance with security baseline (inventoried issues on all devices and systems; we are now addressing these)

Risk mitigation processes are executed to manage risk to an acceptable level.

IP Metrics

Information Protection Measurements-Program Results xx/ xx/ xx		2013	2012	2011	2010
Security Metrics					
Network Security	Network Incidents	6	1	1	1
	Network Attacks	**36,030,760**	**9,237,543**	**1,062,281**	**292,927**
	Virus Infections	2133	216	918	2,329
	Virus/WormAttacks	627,702	436,799	654,603	11,336
	External IP Addresses Scanned	50,573	44,712	13,247	n/a
	High Risk Vulnerabilities Found	380	245	236	n/a
	Internal IP Addresses Scanned	56,827	57,401	*481,835	0
	High Risk Vulnerabilities Found	5,322	4,239	555	0
	Number of Phone Lines Scanned for Modems	225,900	206,297	266,000	264,000
	Modems Found	5,960	6,476	12,841	12,743
	High Risk Modems Found	2	23	23	267
	Wireless Locations Scanned (HQ)	701	673	0	0
	Access Points Found	48	46	0	0
	High Risk Vulnerabilities Found	2	4	0	0
Computer Security	Mission-Critical Systems Measured	1,012	1,194	1,297	304
Application Security	Risk Analysis' Completed	210	414	150	134

*A one-time scan, prompted by Code Red virus, of every IP address to determine those attached to servers or other systems. Scans are now done monthly for IP addresses assigned for use.

200x Initiatives (current year)

- Formed SWAT Team for high-profile focused effort to upgrade and maintain conformity
- Tighten processes and procedures to maintain conformity
  - Enhanced reporting and management focus
  - SOX controls to maintain conformance systems
- Increase automated security (active directory, scripting) and improve tracking
- Expand enterprise disaster recovery
- Institute procedures to ensure that new equipment and capability is in conformance before introduction into our systems
- Review and upgrade objectives, strategy, policies, and procedures for IP
- Continue benchmarking

Conclusion

- IP challenges are growing, and we are growing with them
- We have a comprehensive strategy in place which maintains the integrity and availability of our information resources:
  - Protection
  - Documentation
  - Third-Party Verification (internal and external)
  - Governance
- We have an opportunity to use the structure and discipline provided by Sarbanes-Oxley to augment our IP approach
- We are leveraging the power of our people through awareness and involvement initiatives
- We have upgraded and will continue to improve our management and tracking systems

Information Protection Policies Checklist

WHAT'S HERE

This appendix offers guidance about the policy documents that are often found in large to very large organizations.

HOW TO USE THIS APPENDIX

Review these suggestions and consider them in the context of your organization's policy environment.

EXAMPLE POLICY DOCUMENTS

Policies	Common Examples
Enterprise Information Security Policy	Corporate information security policy
Information Asset Protection	
	Physical and environmental (e.g., hardware, social engineering)
	Identification and authorization
	Remote access protection
	Encryption
	Integrity protection
	Disaster recovery (contingency planning)
	Malware (e.g., anti-virus, anti-spyware)
	Security logging
	Internet infrastructure
	Network protection (e.g., connectivity, Bluetooth, LAN, microwave laser, VOIP, satellite, PBX)
	Access control
	OS and application security
	Information systems backup (data)
	Information systems availability (redundancies)
Site Inspections and Audit	
Information Protection Awareness and Training (new hire, on-going, and third party)	

Information Asset Management		
	Life-cycle management	
	Change control	
Acceptable Use		
	Information privacy (confidentiality)	
	Email and IM use	
	Mobile/wireless device use	
	Telecom use	
	Software use	
	Internet/intranet use (all types of applications, delivery mechanisms, and Internet mediums)	
	Network use	
	Remote access use	
	Misuse reporting	
Incident Management		
	Threat assessment	
	Incident response (investigations)	
	Threat detection and monitoring (intrusion)	
Consequences for Noncompliance		
Roles and Responsibilities		
	Management	
	Business units	
	Employee	
	Security executive	
Classifying, Handling, Receipt, Transmission, Storage, and Destruction (digital and hard form)		
Policy Development and Evaluation Process (Definition: continual updating and review of security policies and procedures)		

EXAMPLE DATA CLASSIFICATION POLICY ELEMENTS

For data classification policy, the security function shall go to the business units and ask what their most confidential and proprietary information is. This will provide examples of commonality of classification. The key is to devote most efforts to protecting critical data. A commonly used classification scheme is:

Public: All information that has been approved by management for public release. Examples include: Media releases, advertisements, and other information developed specifically for distribution outside the company is designated "Public."

Internal Use Only: All internal information that does not meet the criteria for confidential and is to be viewed only by the organization's employees and authorized contractors and other third parties. All information generated within the organization that is not designated as public is considered for internal business use only, and may be released outside of the company only with management approval. This is also known as for official use only.

Confidential: This classification is used for the most sensitive information that must be tightly controlled, even within the organization. Access to information with this classification is strictly on a need-to-know basis or as required by the terms of a contract. Information with this classification may also be referred to as sensitive or proprietary. This information may be released outside of the company only when it is necessary for a specific business objective and the recipient of the information has been bound by a nondisclosure agreement.

Precautions for handling business critical information include:

- Labeling
- Information handling
- Information disposal

Note: Some organizations (primarily government and government contractors) add **Secret** and/or **Top Secret**.

An Example Roles and Responsibilities RACI Matrix

WHAT'S HERE

This appendix offers an example of a Responsibility, Accountability, Consult, and Inform (RACI) matrix for a representative large to very large organization. (Note: RACI matrices were discussed in Information Protection Function One: Governance.)

HOW TO USE THIS APPENDIX

Use this example to generate a specific RACI matrix for your organization. To customize this matrix, first identify the responsibilities (rows) that are part of the IP program, removing or adding to the rows in this example. Then identify the organizational unit (columns) that will be involved in the IP program. Next, determine which of the organizational roles will be performed from a central location (as a headquarters or corporate function) and which ones will be performed in a decentralized manner (e.g., business units, facilities, remote sites). The location should be noted in the column heading.

For each responsibility, assign the proper role to the organizational units. Roles include:

R = Responsible (person or group who is responsible for the implementation)
A = Accountable (person or group who approves decision or action)
C = Consult (person or group consulted about decision or action)
I = Inform (person or group who needs to know about the decision or action)

Each row should have at least one person or group shown as responsible and at least one as accountable. The consult and inform roles are not always present.

We recommend you prepare this matrix using the following process:

- Validate the column headings for the organizational units in your specific organization.
- Validate the row captions to make sure that each responsibility is carried out somewhere in your organization. You will very likely have to add, remove, split, or combine the responsibilities shown here.
- Gather representatives from the units represented by columns in your finalized matrix to function as an expert panel.
- Use a row-wise process to determine the roles for each unit with regard to each responsibility. Record the results of that discussion in the matrix.

EXAMPLE RACI MATRIX

RESPONSIBILITY	Organizational Unit (Each unit is corporate/HQ except as noted)														
	Application Delivery (Divisional)	Audit	Client Liaison Group	Corp. Comm.	Corp. Security	HR	Information Owner	IT Ops (Divisional)	IT Security Group	Legal	Network Ops. (Corp. and Div.)	Procurement	R&D	Security Council	System Owner (Divisional)
1. Setting overall direction and goals; approving IT security policies and initiatives															
2. Monitoring exposure to major threats to information assets															
3. Reviewing and monitoring significant security incidents															
4. Determining outline responses to emerging security threats likely to affect the entire company															
5. Reviewing and agreeing to roles and responsibilities for IT security across the organization															
6. Ensuring there are no gaps in the organization security infrastructure															
7. Review of compliance to IT security legislation (e.g., SOX, data protection) across the organization group															
8. Ensuring that suitable monitoring processes are in place (e.g., risk management around IT security, processes for capturing threat information, etc.)															
9. Ensuring that an independent review of IT security is performed as needed															
10. Providing direction on the balance between risk and business priorities															
11. Ensuring IT security risk analysis s performed on the information at regular intervals (e.g., new business projects, upgrades to systems, etc.)															

Organizational Unit (Each unit is corporate/HQ except as noted)

RESPONSIBILITY	Application Delivery (Divisional)	Audit	Client Liaison Group	Corp. Comm.	Corp. Security	HR	Information Owner	IT Ops (Divisional)	IT Security Group	Legal	Network Ops. (Corp. and Div.)	Procurement	R&D	Security Council	System Owner (Divisional)
12. Maintains responsibility for protecting intellectual property (e.g., formulas, product releases)															
13. Ensuring resolution of issues concerning access privileges and data integrity															
14. Defining the system owner's responsibilities															
15. Setting rules under which an individual should be able to access and modify the information															
16. Determining IT security requirements, (e.g., if the information is confidential)															
17. Ensuring that there are business continuity plans which are tested regularly (e.g., annually)															
18. Considering the risks to the information assets that they and staff use															
19. Developing and maintaining appropriate information control procedures in support of the corporate IT security policies															
20. Ensuring that staff and contractors are aware of security responsibilities and are able to comply with them															
21. Ensuring that there are contingency plans for their area to cover interruptions in the availability of information															
22. Ensuring that all IT security incidents are reported through documented reporting procedures															

23. Ensuring the security of IT assets in their area												
24. Ensuring that security is included in job responsibilities												
25. Allocating the appropriate resources for IT security responsibilities												
26. Ensuring that operating procedures are documented												
27. Ensuring the data protection and privacy of information												
28. Safeguarding of important organizational records (e.g., accounting records, transaction logs, audit logs, operational procedures)												
29. Responsible for compliance with applicable regulations												
30. Provide the IT security group with data to produce metrics to measure compliance (e.g., with SOX legislation)												
31. Keeping third party agreements (TPAs) up to date (e.g., with systems names and access changes)												
32. For each type of access to their system, document potential segregation of duty risks and discuss with the line manager to interpret those risks when assigning access rights over a range of systems to their people												
33. Understanding the security requirements of the information owner and system/app owner (i.e., business department customers)												
34. Consulting with IT security and advising on potential solutions to fulfil business department customers' requirements												
35. Providing cost- effective solutions to defined IT security requirements, as part of providing IT solutions to their business department customers												

Organizational Unit (Each unit is corporate/HQ except as noted)

RESPONSIBILITY	Application Delivery (Divisional)	Audit	Client Liaison Group	Corp. Comm.	Corp. Security	HR	Information Owner	IT Ops (Divisional)	IT Security Group	Legal	Network Ops. (Corp. and Div.)	Procurement	R&D	Security Council	System Owner (Divisional)
36. Ensuring the integrity of application software code that has been purchased															
37. Ensuring that the business departments are aware of the need to protect their information and IT facilities, understand their information IT security responsibilities, and are informed of any IT security issues that may affect their business															
38. Implementing the chosen solution (e.g., assigning resources, producing plans, timescales, costs, etc.)															
39. Influence the business on IT security and business continuity/disaster recovery needs															
40. Ensuring that the simplification of data warehouses/sources is not undermined by disagreements between information owners and system owners															
41. Where ownership of information or business applications is unclear, (i.e., if more than one department shares the information), facilitate the determination of ownership and responsibilities															
42. Ensuring that all security solutions are in place (e.g., have all needed security patches been applied to the operating system) and current virus protection is applied															
43. Developing and maintaining the process for inventory of IT assets															
44. Ensuring that IT equipment (e.g., hardware, software, telecommunications) are properly															

protected, adequate power supplies are available, etc. This includes equipment off-premises and the secure disposal or re-use of equipment														
45. Developing and maintaining the IT security network architectures (which are driven by the IT security policies and standards)														
46. Ensuring that the IT security guidelines are used by developers														
47. Ensuring the secure handover of the application and associated configuration to the production environment														
48. Ensuring that comprehensive testing, including security testing and acceptance testing, has been performed														
49. Ensuring the integrity of application software code that has been developed by IT or provided by IT through third party suppliers														
50. Providing advice and support to the CIO and the director of safety, security, and risk in carrying out their responsibilities for IT security														
51. Developing, maintaining, and evaluating IT security policies, including use of access control, network services, etc.														
52. Promoting formal security risk management practices including identifying threats, vulnerabilities, countermeasures (e.g., access controls, sensitive system isolation and segregation in networks, control of system utilities, encryption, etc.), and business consequences														
53. Performing IT security risk analysis to identify risks from third party access														
54. Ensuring that IT security requirements are included in outsourcing contracts and in third party contracts														

Organizational Unit (Each unit is corporate/HQ except as noted)

RESPONSIBILITY	Application Delivery (Divisional)	Audit	Client Liaison Group	Corp. Comm.	Corp. Security	HR	Information Owner	IT Ops (Divisional)	IT Security Group	Legal	Network Ops. (Corp. and Div.)	Procurement	R&D	Security Council	System Owner (Divisional)
55. Maintaining a central repository to record the IT security risk analysis															
56. Working with Legal to provide advice on legislation, standards, practices, and procedures that affect IT security and standards															
57. Providing IT security specialist advice to the business															
58. Monitoring, measuring, and reporting compliance to the operation of the organization's IT security policies and standards															
59. Monitoring, measuring, and reporting compliance and effective administration of IT security access controls															
60. Monitoring, measuring, and reporting compliance to legislation requirements															
61. Monitoring, measuring, and reporting to ensure there are business continuity/disaster recovery plans in place for IT resources and that they are regularly tested															
62. Developing and implementing enterprise IT security awareness and training programs															
63. Ensuring the development and implementation of enterprise incident management procedures															

64. Assigning and managing the IT security coordinators, data protection coordinators, etc.												
65. Ensuring that information and software exchange agreements include security requirements												
66. Verifying that the personnel screening policy and process, terms and conditions of employment, confidentiality agreements, and a disciplinary process are all in place												
67. Ensuring cooperation between organizations (e.g., law enforcement, authorities, regulatory bodies, information service providers, telecommunication providers, etc.) to be able to quickly deal with security incidents												
68. Ensuring reasonable classification guidelines are defined												
69. Benchmarking against industry												
70. Ensuring a process exists for the collection of IT security evidence												
71. Maintaining the IT business continuity planning framework and management process												
72. Ensuring that outsourced software development follows company standards												
73. Ensuring compliance with IT security policy, including technical compliance checking												
74. Ensuring that all new systems, applications, and other IT elements are in compliance with the security architectures												

Risk Prioritization Procedure Matrix

WHAT'S HERE

This appendix provides a checklist of some of the risks that are often found in large and very large organizations. Risks are categorized as high (H), medium (M), or low (L) according to their likelihood and potential impact.

HOW TO USE THIS APPENDIX

Review this matrix to develop a specific list of risks for your organization. First, check to see if the risks present in your organization are listed in rows in the table. Then revise the columns to be complete and accurate for the specifics found in your organization's specific environment (for example, a threat listed below as a high risk may in fact be considered a low risk to your organization).

RISK PRIORITIZATION MATRIX

Risk	Threats	Vulnerabilities	Potential Business Consequences	Countermeasures
H	• Malicious code • Denial Of Service (DoS) • Distributed DoS (DDOS) • Mobile code • Spoofing • Sniffing • Eavesdropping • Masquerading	• System/devices with no antivirus protection software • System/devices with outdated virus definition file • Vendor softwaredeficiencies (SANS/FBI's TopWindows, UNIX, and Linux vulnerabilities) • Software bugs (those that compromise security) • Unpatched systems/ devices • Undocumented hardware installations (e.g., wireless devices), due to poor policies	• Processing delays due to system outage (e.g., DoS) • Additional labor required to restore system or data • Opens door for potential loss or corruption of or unauthorized access to sensitive and/or critical data • Unauthorized use and/or malicious use of IT resources • Interruption of process control systems that are monitored and controlled by Windows, UNIX, or	1. Policies, standards, and procedures 2. Vulnerability analysis 3. Patch management 4. Configuration management 5. Virus protection 6. Change management 7. Security awareness and training

	"and procedures regarding addition of network equipment • Poor account and password management • Sensitive/confidential information sent via the Internet or not encrypted while in storage	LINUX (inability to get the product out the door) • Disclosure of information to unauthorized persons • Destruction of information or of hardware/equipment • Unavailability of information, software, hardware/equipment, and telecommunications • Modification or alteration of information, software, and information systems • Theft of information or equipment		
H	• Remote access users (employees, business partners, customers, consultants, and contractors plugging into network with their own computer devices)	• No antivirus or patterns not up-to-date • Poorly configured or unpatched system • Poor account and password management	• Opens door for potential loss or corruption of, or unauthorized access to, sensitive and/or critical data • Processing delays due to system outage • Additional labor required to restore system or data	1. Policies, standards, and procedures 2. Virus protection 3. Configuration and patch management 4. Security awareness and training 5. Change management 6. Inventory system 7. Protection for portable device/home user 8. Locking mechanisms for docking stations 9. Tracing software 10. Encryption software
L	• Unauthorized software	• Unauthorized software download for personal use or workplace use • Embedded malicious code	• Commercial software piracy (copyright infringement) • Workstation unavailable due to session "hijacking" • Disclosure of information to unauthorized persons	1. Policies, standards, and procedures 2. Configuration management 3. Security awareness and training 4. Virus management 5. Remove user administrative access rights to install software
H	• Natural and/or environmental (e.g., earthquakes, floods, storms, hurricanes, and fires)	• People • Property • The environment	• Sick, missing people • Destroyed/damaged property • Destroyed/damaged environment	1. Have an incident response plan (IRP) and exercise it regularly 2. Fire protection (reduce cause of fire); detection (receive warnings before it becomes a problem); and suppression (how to contain and extinguish fire to minimize damage) 3. Water pipes and fire-suppression system; make sure data center or server room is not located next to or directly below sources of water

				4. In flood plain, don't put critical information systems in first floor or basement
H	• Supply systems (e.g., power outages, communications outages)	• People • Computers and information	• Sick and/or frightened people • Computer cannot operate due to over-heating/and or lack of power	1. Electric power surge suppressors prevent sudden surges or spikes by acting as a clamp at the supply box and/or uninterruptible power supply (UPS) provides continuous power in the event of an outage 2. HVAC and refrigeration (HVACR) for data center independent of the rest of the building
H	• Human-made (e.g., theft, vandalism, explosions)	• People • Computers and information • Property	• People unable to work due to psychological effects • Critical asset/information loss	1. Perimeter and building grounds security 2. Surveillance devices 3. Building entry points 4. Compartmentalized areas
M	• Physical or logical accidents and disasters	• Lack of documented and tested disaster recovery plans	• Inability to recover systems timely/processing delays; potential loss or corruption of data	1. Disaster recovery planning and testing 2. Data center or server room security

Security Awareness and Training Menu

WHAT'S HERE

This appendix offers a list of frequently used awareness and training methods and a menu of potential awareness and training topics for consideration in your organization.

HOW TO USE THIS APPENDIX

Consider the training methods and content options presented here for use at your organization.

SECURITY AWARENESS AND TRAINING DELIVERY METHODS

Dissemination Methods (continually used):	Additional Materials:
Classroom training	Posters
Management development	Handbooks or brochures
New employee orientation	Computer-delivered clips
Screen savers	Formal presentations
Intranet	Corporate newsletter
Staff meetings	Handouts
Email alerts	Awareness awards
Lunch-and-learn programs	Policies
Posters	Videos
Security newsletters	
Computer-based training modules	

SECURITY AWARENESS AND TRAINING MENU

Topic	What Needs to Be Communicated
Cyberterrorism (e.g., viruses, hacking, DoS)	• Virus protection software usage • Email attachment vulnerabilities
Data back up and storage	• When and how to back up • Preferred storage methodology
How and when to report and respond to threats	• Reporting structure in case of incident or suspected incident
Internet/intranet	• Email/IM protocols • Internet usage
Laptops and other mobile equipment	• Log-off/lock-down • Securing equipment • Reporting when lost or stolen • Business vs. personal use
Legal use of software	• Software and copyright law • Embedded malicious software threats
Passwords	• Strong passwords • Memorize passwords • Do not share passwords
Policies and compliance	• What and where policies are located • Specific regulatory requirements • Consequences when fail to comply
Privacy (identity theft)	• Employee data • Customer data
Propriety information protection	• Usage of classification scheme • Document retention schedule • Communal equipment usage • Shredding
Roles and responsibilities	• Who is responsible for what
Social engineering/industrial espionage	• Answering phone calls • Answering emails • Sending faxes • Clear desk policy • Access control (e.g., passwords) • ID passes • Off-site meetings • Using PCs and laptops • Visitor access
Wireless security risks	• Change default password/SSID • Encryption—Personal firewalls

Risk Assessment and Compliance Checklist

WHAT'S HERE

This self-assessment tool and audit benchmark is designed to assess information security management practices using a framework of 102 security objectives. It is a compilation of common practices from standards (ISO 27002) and audit documentation from exemplary companies (see the Acknowledgments section for more information about which companies contributed audit documentation).

HOW TO USE THIS APPENDIX

Consider the specific risk elements in your organization and adapt this checklist to your organization's specific needs.

1. After a self-assessment checklist is developed that is specific to your information protection program needs, review the checklist with your audit and/or compliance functions to obtain feedback on missing controls, and inform them what they should audit against.
2. Train the business units on the self-assessment checklist, how it is used in the auditing process, and the process for implementation of both data collection and the radiation action plan that follows.
3. Monitor, review, and give feedback. Charts and graphics give clear indication of status.

RISK ASSESSMENT AND COMPLIANCE CHECKLIST

Cover Sheet and Instructions

Business unit	<Business unit>
Name of BU head	<name>
Name of IT director*	<name>
Name of information security coordinator	<name>
Period covered	DD/MM/YYYY to DD/MM/YYYY
Date completed	DD/MM/YYYY

* IT director sign-off is for the summary and sections four through seven only

This tool implements the following risk assessment framework
RISK = PROBABILITY * IMPACT
[Threats x (Vulnerabilities – Countermeasures)] *   Business Consequences

Threats are classified as external (e.g., hackers, worms, viruses), internal (e.g., employees, contractors), and natural (e.g., hurricanes, tornadoes, floods, lightning, fire). Tools such as this one are needed to identify threats and vulnerabilities. The vulnerabilities and threats that lead to significant impact to the business are mitigated via the implementation of the appropriate countermeasures.

Once the PROBABILITY [Threats x (Vulnerabilities - Countermeasures)] is identified, the IMPACT (i.e., the business consequences) to the organization can be determined.

Steps for assessment completion:

1. The impact assessment (IA) is performed and pre–filled by the information security group for each major control (e.g., governance).
2. For each control (e.g., responsibilities for information security are clearly defined), the business unit completes:
    a) Existing controls (e.g., information security responsibilities are documented for the IT groups);
    b) Future mitigating actions (e.g., information security responsibilities will be documented for the business units);
    c) Owner and date; and
    d) Compliance score [0 – 5 as documented under **Compliance Score (COMPL) Score** below].
3. Based on the answers given to each major control (e.g., organizational security), the business unit completes:
    a) The residual impact assessment (RIA), and
    b) The probability assessment (PA).
    Do this by using one of the codes as listed below under residual impact assessment (RIA) and probability assessment (PA).
4. At the end of the form, please complete the summary:
    a) Risk appetite (RA) using the definitions under **Risk Appetite (RA)** below, and
    b) Summarize the key issues in the box provided.

Impact Assessment (IA)	**Residual Impact Assessment (RIA)**	**Probability Assessment (PA)**
1 – Catastrophic 2 – Critical 3 – Significant 4 – Important	1 – Catastrophic 2 – Critical 3 – Significant 4 – Important	1 – Likely 2 – Possible 3 – Remote 4 – Extremely remote

Compliance (COMPL) Score	**Risk Appetite (RA)**
5 – Fully implemented 4 – Partially implemented 3 – Planned in the next few weeks or months 2 – Planned in the future 1 – Not planned 0 – Not applicable	**UR – Unacceptable Risk (Red)** **VR – Volatile Risk (Amber)** **AMA – Acceptable Mitigating Actions (Yellow)** **AR – Acceptable Risk (Green)**

1. GOVERNANCE		
Impact Assessment	**Control**	
Critical	**Risk:** Inadequate governance leads to unmanaged/uncontrolled risk.	
Control	**Existing Controls**	**Future Mitigating Actions**
1.1. Roles and Responsibilities		
1.1.1. Responsibilities for information security are clearly defined.		
1.1.2. An authorization process for the installation, implementation, or upgrading of IT facilities is established.		

2. ASSET CRITICALITY CLASSIFICATION		
Impact Assessment	**Control**	
Significant	**Risk:** Inadequate controls over sensitive assets may result in unauthorized disclosure. Lack of asset control results can make it impossible to recover in the event of a disaster.	
Control	**Existing Controls**	**Future Mitigating Actions**
2.1. Identification and Registration		
2.1.1. An inventory of all important information assets is maintained.		
2.1.2. Information asset owners are identified and are responsible for the asset's maintenance and protection.		
2.2. Information Classification		
2.2.1. Information which, if disclosed, would result in major monetary losses or major damage to reputation, has been identified and is classified as **Confidential.**		
2.2.2. Information for release to the public is vetted by an authorized manager (before its release) to ensure accuracy and appropriateness for public consumption.		
2.3. Risk Management		
2.3.1. An information losses business impact assessment is undertaken as part of the systems development life cycle and for all systems with **Confidential** information.		

3. SECURITY AWARENESS & TRAINING		
Impact Assessment	**Control**	
Critical	**Risk:** Inadequate personnel controls (hiring, training, and awareness) may result in accidental or deliberate misuse of information or systems.	
Control	**Existing Controls**	**Future Mitigating Actions**
3.1. Recruitment		
3.1.1. Human resources has ensured recruitment procedures are put into place which verify the identity, qualifications, ability, and suitability (e.g. character, credit status) of new employees.		
3.2. Awareness and Training		
3.2.1. All staff members have signed a confidentiality agreement recognizing the organization's ownership of information and restricting its disclosure or dissemination to authorized persons (this may form part of the employee contract).		
3.2.2. All staff are regularly advised of the need for security, of what are acceptable and unacceptable practices, and of their own responsibilities for complying with security polices.		
3.2.3. Training is provided to a level that ensures staff members are able to correctly use IT facilities and safeguard information assets.		
3.2.4. Failures to comply with information security policies are dealt with through a formal disciplinary process.		

4. PHYSICAL ACCESS CONTROLS		
Impact Assessment	**Control**	
Catastrophic	**Risk:** Inadequate physical controls may result in damage to the business through unauthorized disclosure, modification, or loss (permanent or temporary) to data and systems.	
Control	**Existing Controls**	**Future Mitigating Actions**
4.1. Physical Assets		
4.1.1. Information systems supporting critical or sensitive business activities are located in secure areas to which only authorized personnel have access.		
4.1.2. Sensitive or critical information and other business materials are secured when not in use, especially outside normal working hours.		
4.1.3. All individual items of equipment are subject to controls designed to reduce the potential for loss or damage.		
4.1.4. Equipment is protected from physical security threats and environmental hazards, e.g., fire, smoke, water, dust, etc.		

4.1.5. Equipment is maintained in accordance with suppliers' recommendations and maintenance is carried out by authorized personnel.		
4.1.6. Measures have been taken to prevent sensitive corporate or personal information being compromised when physically transferring data off premises, sending equipment off premises for maintenance, or disposing of equipment.		

5. OPERATIONS CHANGE MANAGEMENT		
Impact Assessment	**Control**	
Catastrophic	**Risk:** Inadequate communication and operations controls can lead to compromise in confidentiality of information, and damage to the infrastructure.	
Control	**Existing Controls**	**Future Mitigating Actions**
5.1. Operations and Support		
5.1.1. Clear documented operating procedures have been prepared for all aspects of IT systems operation, maintenance, and support.		
5.1.2. Incident management responsibilities and procedures have been established to ensure a fast, effective, and orderly response to security incidents.		
5.2. Change Control and Maintenance		
5.2.1. Detection and prevention controls to protect against malicious software (e.g., viruses, Trojan horses, etc.) have been implemented.		
5.2.2. An effective change control system has been defined and implemented across all areas.		
5.3. Network Management		
5.3.1. Technologies including firewalls, proxy servers, and routers have been employed to enforce access control policies.		
5.3.2. A firewall is used to control communications between internal company networks and external public (e.g., Internet) networks.		
5.3.3. PBX systems or other systems that may be used for voice communications are defined and supported in accordance with the same security principles as those used for data communications.		

6. COMPUTER ACCESS CONTROL		
Impact Assessment	**Control**	
Catastrophic	**Risk:** Inadequate access control can lead to authorized and untraceable activity within applications and the infrastructure, potentially leading to fraud and theft.	
Control	**Existing Controls**	**Future Mitigating Actions**
6.1. General		
6.1.1. The access control requirements of each system have been defined by the relevant business owner.		
6.1.2. There is a formal user registration and de-registration process for access to all IT services.		
6.1.3. Passwords are allocated and managed through a formal process.		
6.1.4. Users are provided with help and advice for the selection and protection of passwords (e.g., via awareness literature or electronic support).		
6.1.5. Users are aware that they should ensure that unattended equipment has appropriate protection.		
6.1.6. "Power" accounts are managed.		
6.2. Mobile Computing		
6.2.1. Users have been given specific guidelines for the use and protection of mobile equipment.		
6.2.2. The use of handheld equipment is carefully controlled to ensure personal usage does not compromise company information.		
6.3. Teleworking and Remote Access		
6.3.1. Teleworking and remote access is only allowed following a risk assessment and the implementation of appropriate verification and data protection measures.		
6.3.2. Teleworkers are given guidance on the types of information they may hold on the equipment they use and the specific measures they will need to take for its protection.		
6.3.3. Procedures are in place to ensure a full record is kept of equipment used by teleworkers, and that this equipment is returned when no longer needed.		
6.4. Third-Party Access		
6.4.1. Access to the organization's IT facilities by a third party is not allowed unless there is a written agreement between the organization and the third party on how, when, and why the access has been granted.		

7. SYSTEMS CHANGE MANAGEMENT

Impact Assessment	Control
Significant	**Risk:** Poor controls in the development lifecycle process can result in inadequate or inappropriate controls, leading to accidental or deliberate loss of information or systems.

Control	Existing Controls	Future Mitigating Actions
7.1. Systems Design		
7.1.1. An analysis of security requirements is carried out at the design and requirements specification stage of any systems development project.		
7.1.2. Systems are designed to provide users with assurance of the continuing accuracy and protection of data entered.		
7.1.3. E-Commerce applications receive rigorous testing to ensure that back-end systems remain intact and that any errors in front-end systems are low profile.		
7.2. Testing		
7.2.1. The use of live data for testing is strictly controlled to prevent unauthorized amendment and disclosure.		

8. BUSINESS CONTINUITY MANAGEMENT

Impact Assessment	Control
Catastrophic	**Risk:** Inadequate business continuity planning and testing can undermine the ability of the business to recover from an incident.

Control	Existing Controls	Future Mitigating Actions
8.1. Planning Process		
8.1.1. Business managers consider the need for business continuity plans and, where appropriate, develop mechanisms for ensuring that operational work can be resumed/ continued if key elements of the computers or information systems upon which they rely become unavailable.		
8.1.2. An up-to-date inventory of each application system and its criticality to the business is maintained.		

9. COMPUTER ACCESS CONTROL			
Impact Assessment	**Control**		
Catastrophic	**Risk:** Legal and regulatory noncompliance can result in legal action against the business or even suspension of license to do business.		
Control		**Existing Controls**	**Future Mitigating Actions**
9.1 Legal Requirements			
9.1.1. To avoid breaches of statutory, criminal, or civil obligations, steps are taken to ensure compliance with all aspects of legislation and other regulations affecting the use of information and information systems.			
9.1.2. Intellectual property rights relating to the use of data and information including software, publications (electronic or hard copy), music, and videos are enforced and protected.			
9.1.3. Important company records are protected against loss, destruction, or falsification in accordance with relevant legislation.			
9.1.4. Controls have been put in place to ensure the protection of personal data relating to identifiable individuals in accordance with Group ethics policies and relevant local legislation.			
9.1.5. Users have been given precise information regarding their scope of access and use of IT facilities.			
9.1.6. Departments with operational responsibilities for monitoring email and Internet systems have formally documented rules and procedures.			
9.2. Internal Audit and Governance			
9.2.1. To ensure compliance with information security policy and standards, periodic reviews including formal audit are completed regularly.			
9.2.2. Actions to investigate possible staff misuse or abuse of email or Internet systems are taken only under specifically authorized circumstances.			

SUMMARY					
Impact Assessment	**Key Issues**	**Key Actions**	**RA**	**RIA**	**PA**
Catastrophic	RISK: Lack of security over information and/or applications negatively impacts the business, e.g. fraud, theft, loss of confidentiality, loss of integrity, loss of availability.		?	2.6	2.4
		Residual Impact Score — Probability Score —			
		Compliance Score — Compliance % Score —	120	47%	
Please summarize your identified key issues in the rows below					
	<enter text here>				

Incident Response

WHAT'S HERE

The flowcharts provided here first diagram the process used to create contingency plans for incident response, and then illustrate the steps involved in an incident reaction.

HOW TO USE THIS APPENDIX

Refer to these flowcharts as you develop and execute plans to create or revise your contingency planning processes.

INCIDENT RESPONSE PLANNING

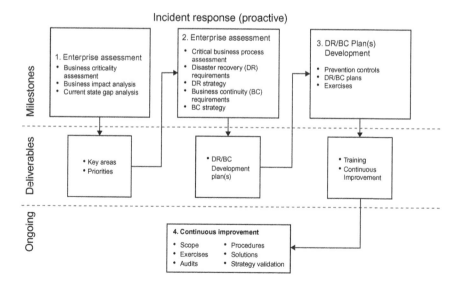

INCIDENT REACTION

Incident response

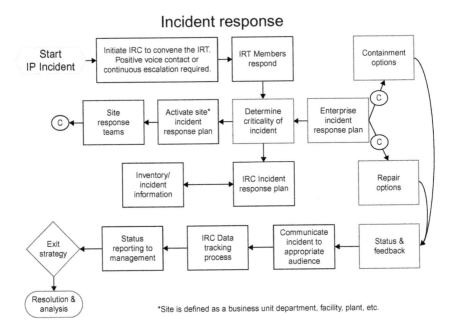

*Site is defined as a business unit department, facility, plant, etc.

Facility Management Self-Assessment

WHAT'S HERE

The self-assessment questionnaire can be used to quickly identify gaps in security controls at lower cost and effort than full security audits.

HOW TO USE THIS APPENDIX

Successful implementation of information protection measures is characterized by consistent application of measures to limit unauthorized access to company information. The information security coordinator or another designate should establish self-assessment mechanisms to periodically review the effectiveness of the organization's information security program.

An example of a self-assessment mechanism would be to conduct after-hours reviews to determine whether workstations are being cleared of confidential materials at the end of the business day. Incidents of noncompliance could result in a reminder notice to the responsible employee.

Consider the specific risk elements in your organization and adapt this checklist to your organization's specific needs.

SELF-ASSESSMENT QUESTIONNAIRE

1. Is access to the facility adequately controlled? Are visitors signed in and escorted?
2. Are employees complying with the corporate badging policies and standards?
3. Are work areas cleared of confidential information at the end of the workday?
4. Do employees have adequate lockable storage?
5. Do employees with home offices follow the policy and measures?

6. Are procedures in place for disposing of sensitive waste?
7. Are safeguards in place to reduce chances of misdirected fax transmissions? Are fax machines cleared of sent and received faxes at the end of the workday?
8. Are employees aware of proper telephone procedures and how to handle suspicious inquiries?
9. Are employees who use cellular and cordless telephones aware of precautions to be taken when using these devices?
10. Do all employees within the organization understand that information is a valuable corporate asset and that they are responsible for using information for business purposes only?
11. Is information being managed so that it is released only when time and conditions are favorable for the organization?
12. Are employees aware of which information in the organization is considered confidential?
13. Are consistent and effective controls established over all computer systems used within the organization, including individual accountability and password controls?
14. Are adequate physical controls in place so that unauthorized individuals do not have access to business critical information or systems (e.g., access to the data center)?

Roles in Information Protection

WHAT'S HERE

This appendix offers representative job descriptions relevant to information protection. The job descriptions are excerpted from an upcoming Elsevier publication, *Security Careers*, written by Steven Walker and James Foushée of the Foushée Group, a management consulting firm specializing in compensation program design and research and a leading provider of security and compliance compensation information to organizations.

HOW TO USE THIS APPENDIX

The structure of the management team and the individual position descriptions are widely variable across the information protection landscape. The following are representative samples of some of the positions frequently found in information protection roles.

EXAMPLE POSITIONS

Top Global Security Executive

Job Description: This is the most senior executive security position in the organization with direct line responsibility. This position has global accountability for developing and directing the organization security program.

- Directs the domestic and international staff in identifying, developing, implementing, and maintaining security processes across the organization to reduce risks, respond to incidents, and limit exposure to liability in all areas of financial, physical, network/information technology, and personal risk.
- Coordinates and implements site security, operations, and activities to ensure the protection of executives, managers, employees, and

physical and information assets while ensuring the optimal use of personnel and equipment.

- Develops and delivers service in response to criminal financial loss, counterfeiting, crimes against persons, sabotage, threats, emergencies, illegal acts, and property or environmental crimes.
- Accountable for state-of-the-art technology solutions and innovative security management techniques to safeguard the organization's assets and correct security vulnerabilities with new and legacy IT systems.
- May be responsible for ensuring the safety of all network and information system environments for the corporation and operating business units.
- Incumbent may be responsible for network/IS technical security architecture, network and system designs, and implementation and management of systems and programs for the prevention of system hacking and virus protection.
- Develops and implements intrusion detection systems to prevent abuse and virus release within the organization.
- Establishes appropriate standards and risk controls associated with intellectual property.
- Develops standards and policies worldwide for compliance with government rules, regulations, laws, and treaties regarding security requirements for import and export of products.
- Directs the approach, deployment, and execution of the most sensitive investigations. Develops relationships with high-level law enforcement and international counterparts to include in-country security and international security agencies and intelligence and private sector counterparts worldwide.
- Develops consensus within an organization from operational activities and regulations imposed by agencies with regulatory jurisdiction.

Qualification Guidelines: Master's degree or international equivalent in an area of study relevant to this position and more than 20 years of experience with a major corporation and/or law enforcement, intelligence, or public or private sector security organization, or bachelor's degree or international equivalent in an area of study relevant to this position and more than 25 years of experience with a major corporation and/or law enforcement, intelligence, or public or private sector security organization. Has demonstrated experience and exposure in the international security arena.

Global Security Executive

Job Description: This is the most senior security management position of a major operating unit (sector, group, or large division) level. This position can have domestic and international security accountabilities for the operating unit.

- Directs the development and implementation the operating unit's security policies and programs.
- Directs the domestic and international staff in identifying, developing, implementing, and maintaining security processes across the operating unit to reduce risks, respond to incidents, and limit exposure to liability in order to reduce financial loss to the organization.
- Identifies significant security risks and designs and implements strategies and programs to prevent and reduce loss of the organization's assets.
- Establishes appropriate standards and risk controls associated with intellectual property within the operating unit.
- Directs, coordinates, and implements site security, operations, and activities to ensure the protection of executives, managers, employees, and physical and information assets while ensuring optimal use of personnel and equipment.
- Develops and delivers preventative programs and services to protect against criminal financial loss, counterfeiting, crime against persons, sabotage, threats, emergencies, illegal acts, and property or environmental crimes.
- Researches and deploys state-of-the-art technology solutions and innovative security management techniques to safeguard the operating unit's assets.
- Directs the approach, deployment, and execution of investigations, and directs team-based systems development efforts.
- Develops and manages the capital and expense budget for the unit's worldwide security operations.
- Develops close relationships with high-level law enforcement and international counterparts to include in-country security and international security agencies, intelligence and private sector counterparts worldwide.
- Briefs executive management on status of security issues.
- Develops a consensus position within an organization climate of diverse operational activities and often-conflicting regulations imposed by agencies with regulatory jurisdiction.

- Provides leadership direction to the management and professional staff within the organization unit.

Qualification Guidelines: Master's degree or international equivalent in an area of study relevant to this position and more than 15 years of experience with a major law enforcement, intelligence, public service, or private sector security organization, or bachelor's degree or international equivalent in an area of study relevant to this position and more than 20 years of experience with a major law enforcement, intelligence, or public or private sector security organization. Has demonstrated experience and exposure in the international security arena.

Top Security Executive, Domestic

Job Description: This is the most senior domestic security management position in the organization with direct line responsibility. This position is accountable for developing, implementing, and directing a responsible domestic security program for the organization.

- Directs the security staff in identifying, developing, implementing, and maintaining security processes across the organization to reduce risks, respond to incidents, and limit exposure to liability in order to reduce financial loss to the organization.
- Identifies significant security risks, and designs and implements strategies and programs to prevent/reduce loss of organization assets. Implements risk reduction through increased security awareness.
- Through subordinate managers, coordinates and implements site security, operations, and activities to ensure protection of executives, managers, employees, and physical and information assets, while ensuring optimal use of personnel and equipment.
- Develops and ensures services in response to criminal financial loss, crimes against persons, sabotage, threats, emergencies, illegal acts, and property or environmental crimes.
- May be responsible for ensuring the safety of all network and information system environments for the corporation and operating business units.
- Incumbent may be responsible for network/IS technical security architecture and network and system designs and the implementation and management of systems and programs for the prevention of system hacking and virus protection.

- Develops and implements intrusion detection systems to prevent abuse and virus release within the organization.
- Researches and deploys state-of-the-art technology solutions and innovative security management techniques to safeguard organization assets.
- Directs the approach, deployment, and execution of investigations.
- Develops and manages the capital and expense budget for the unit's domestic security operations.
- Develops close relationships with high-level domestic law enforcement and international counterparts to include in-country security.

Qualification Guidelines: Master's degree in an area of study relevant to this position and more than 15 years of experience with a major corporation and/or law enforcement, intelligence, public service, or private sector security organization, or bachelor's degree or international equivalent in an area of study relevant to this position and more than 20 years of experience with a major law enforcement, intelligence, or public or private sector security organization. Has had exposure in the international security arena.

Director, Computer, Network, and Information Security
Job Description: Plans, directs, and manages the computer, network, and information security function within the organization to ensure its effective operation based on predetermined goals and objectives under executive management direction

- Accountable for the business strategies associated with the technology needed in the security function within the organization.
- Develops and implements the policies, procedures, and systems required for maintaining and enhancing the overall security goals.
- Responsible for the research, design, development, and implementation of the organization's security and protection technologies for computer systems and applications.
- Responsible for the development of security plans, designs, best practices, and guidelines for existing or new technologies within network security and firewall protection.
- Researches, develops, maintains, and audits the analytical and technical aspects of major information and intellectual capital security systems and subsystems.

- Responsible for maintaining and upgrading the security integrity of computer workstations, servers, local area networks, application systems, and software.
- Develops security solutions for the company's virtual private networks, key public infrastructures, authentication, and directory services.
- Accountable for the selection, testing, installation, and operation of cryptographic equipment; securing transmission of classified information and sensitive unclassified information; and the protection of cryptographic principles and methods.
- Accountable for and directs complex surveillance of computer/network protection measures, and creates measurement tools for system vulnerability assessments.
- Researches, develops, contacts, and selects vendors to develop technical solutions for site security needs and presents recommendations to executive management.
- Briefs executive management on major accomplishments, issues, and concerns.
- Responsible for the selecting and developing of key security personnel for the computer, network, and information function of the organization.

Qualification Guidelines: PhD in computer science and more than seven years of experience; master's degree and more than 10 years; or bachelor's degree and more than 15 years of experience or other studies relevant to this position and/or in a major corporation and/or law enforcement, intelligence, or public or private sector security organization. Has exposure in the international security arena. Certified Information Systems Security Professional (CISSP) preferred.

Manager, Computer and Information Security

Job Description: Plans, develops, and directs the computer and information security function under senior management direction.

- Responsible for the business strategies associated with the computer and information security function within the organization.
- Accountable for overall planning, directing, and organizing activities of the computer and information security function, and ensures its effective operation. Implements the policies, procedures, and

systems required for maintaining and enhancing the overall computer and information security organizational mission.

- Responsible for the research, design, development, and implementation of computer security/protection technologies for the organization's information and process systems/applications.
- Accountable for the computer security for classified information security and communications security.
- Researches, contacts, and selects vendors to develop technical solutions for site computer security needs, and presents recommendations to senior management.
- Develops, maintains, and audits the analytical and technical aspects of major computer security subsystems.
- Maintains the integrity of computer workstations, servers, local area networks, upgrading systems, and software for the company.
- Responsible for the selection, testing, and secure installation and operation of cryptographic equipment; securing transmission of classified information and sensitive unclassified information; and the protection of cryptographic principles and methods.
- Responsible for identifying and mitigating threats and vulnerabilities associated with compromising electromagnetic emanations from equipment used to process classified information.
- Develops and provides technical support, training, and timely computer system data recovery to end-users.
- Directs the investigation of computer security incidents, and develops facility protection plans.
- Directs complex surveillance of computer protection measures, and creates measurement tools for system vulnerability assessments.
- Keeps senior management informed on major accomplishments, issues, and concerns.
- Develops, trains, and directs computer and information security personnel within the organization.

Qualification Guidelines: Master's degree in computer science or other studies relevant to this position and more than six years of experience in a major corporation and/or law enforcement, intelligence, public service, or private sector security organization, or bachelor's degree in computer science or other studies relevant to this position and more than 10 years of experience with a major law enforcement, intelligence, or public or private sector security organization. Has had some exposure in the international security arena. Certified Information Systems Security Professional (CISSP) preferred.

Senior Computer and Information Security Specialist IV
Job Description:

- Works under consultative direction toward predetermined goals and objectives.
- Assignments are usually self-initiated.
- Determines and pursues courses of action necessary to obtain desired results, and makes recommendations and changes to departmental policies and procedures. Work is checked through consultation and agreement, rather than formal review of supervisor.
- Responsible for the research, design, development, and implementation of computer security/protection technologies for company information and process systems/applications. Also is accountable for the computer security for classified information security and communications security.
- Acts as lead contact with vendors to develop technical solutions for site computer security needs, and makes recommendations to senior management.
- Develops, maintains, and audits the analytical and technical aspects of major computer security subsystems.
- Maintains integrity of computer workstations, servers, and local area networks by maintaining user accounts and upgrading systems and software as required.
- Responsible for secure installation and operation of cryptographic equipment, secure transmission of classified information and sensitive unclassified information, and protection of cryptographic principles and methods.
- Identifies and mitigates threats and vulnerabilities associated with compromising electromagnetic emanations from equipment used to process classified information.
- Provides technical support, training, and timely computer system data recovery to end-users.
- Oversees the investigation of computer security incidents, and acts as lead analyst of computer facility protection plans.
- Conducts complex surveillance of computer protection measures, and creates measurement tools for system vulnerability assessments.

- Serves on internal committees to represent computer security interests.
- Provides leadership to less experienced computer and information security specialists and technicians.

Qualification Guidelines: Master's degree in computer science or other studies relevant to this position and more than four years of experience in a major corporation and/or law enforcement, intelligence, public service, or private sector security organization, or bachelor's degree in computer science or other studies relevant to this position and more than eight years of experience with a major law enforcement, intelligence, or public or private sector security organization. Exposure in the international security arena is desirable. Certified Information Systems Security Professional (CISSP) preferred.

Computer and Information Security Specialist III
Job Description:

- Works under very limited direction.
- Exercises reasonable latitude in determining computer and information security techniques to accomplish objectives.
- Work is reviewed upon completion for adequacy in meeting objectives.
- Conducts research and designs, develops, and implements computer security/protection technologies for the organization's information and process systems/applications.
- Researches and implements computer security for classified information security and communications security.
- Works with vendors to develop technical solutions for site security needs.
- Conducts maintenance and subsequent audits of the analytical and technical aspects of major computer security subsystems within established guidelines.
- Maintains integrity of computer workstations, servers, and local area networks by maintaining user accounts and recommending upgrades to systems and software required.
- Assists in the secure installation and operation of cryptographic equipment, secure transmission of classified information and sensitive unclassified information, and protection of cryptographic principles and methodologies.

- Works to identify and mitigate threats and vulnerabilities associated with compromising electromagnetic emanations from equipment used to process classified information.
- Provides technical support, training, and timely computer system data recovery to end-users.
- Investigates computer security incidents, and recommends corrective actions.
- Conducts surveillance of computer protection measures, and creates measurement tools for system vulnerability assessments.
- Provides oversight to the client group on appropriate procedures for computer/system security.
- Provides leadership to less experienced computer and information security specialists and technicians.
- May act as lead person or technical expert on medium to large projects.

Qualification Guidelines: Master's degree in computer science or other studies relevant to this position and more than three years of experience with a major corporation and/or law enforcement, intelligence, or public or private sector security organization, or bachelor's degree in computer science or other studies relevant to this position and more than six years of experience with a major law enforcement, intelligence, or public or private sector security organization. Some exposure in the international security arena is desirable. Certified Information Systems Security Professional (CISSP) preferred.

Computer and Information Security Specialist II
Job Description:

- Works is performed under general supervision.
- Follows established procedures.
- Work is reviewed systematically through completion for adequacy in meeting objectives.
- With guidance, conducts research and designs, develops, and implements computer security and protection technologies for organization's information and process systems/applications.
- Assists in the research and implementation of computer security for classified information security and communications security.

- Works with vendors to develop technical solutions for site security needs.
- Maintains integrity of computer workstations, servers, and local area networks by maintaining user accounts and recommending upgrades to systems and software required.
- Responds to client requests, and prepares security plans and reports based on client needs.
- Supports the secure installation and operation of cryptographic equipment, secure transmission of classified information and sensitive unclassified information and protection of cryptographic principles and methodologies.
- Provides technical support to system users to include hardware configuration, installation, diagnostics, testing, problem resolution, system maintenance, and data recovery.
- Assists in the investigation of computer security incidents, and may recommend corrective actions.
- Acts as alternate team lead on small computer security incidents.
- Conducts technical evaluations of hardware, software, and installed systems and networks.
- Conducts certification testing of installed systems to ensure protection strategies are properly implemented.

Qualification Guidelines: Bachelor's degree in computer science or other studies relevant to this position and more than four years of experience with a law enforcement, intelligence, or public or private sector security organization. Certified Information Systems Security Professional (CISSP) preferred.

Computer and Information Security Specialist I
Job Description:

- Works under close supervision.
- Performs tasks from detailed instructions and established procedures.
- Work is reviewed for soundness of technical judgment and for following the defined policies and procedures.
- Under direction of senior staff, evaluates, designs, and develops computer security/protection technologies for company information and process systems/applications.

- May assist in the implementation of computer security for classified information security and communications security.
- Maintains integrity of computer workstations, servers, and local area networks by maintaining user accounts and recommending upgrades to systems and software required.
- Responds to client requests, documenting and reporting any security incidents.
- Provides technical support to system users to include hardware configuration, installation, diagnostics, testing, maintenance, and data recovery.
- Investigates routine computer incidents under direction of a senior specialist.
- Assists in conducting technical evaluations of hardware, software, and installed systems and networks.
- Conducts routine certification testing of installed systems to ensure protection strategies are properly implemented.

Qualification Guidelines: Bachelor's degree in computer science or other studies relevant to this position and a minimum of two years of experience with a law enforcement, intelligence, or public or private sector security organization.

Manager, Network Security
Job Description: Plans, develops, and directs the computer network security function under senior management direction.

- Responsible for the business strategies associated with the computer network security function within the organization.
- Accountable for overall planning, directing, and organizing activities of the computer network security function and ensures its effective operation.
- Implements the policies, procedures, and systems required for maintaining and enhancing the overall computer network security organizational mission.
- Accountable for the research, design, development, and implementation of extremely complex computer network security/protection technologies for company information and network systems/applications.
- Accountable for the development of security plans, designs, best practices, and guidelines for existing or new technologies within network security and firewall protection.

- Develops virus protection security procedures to insure that email and email attachments are appropriately scanned and all network-attachment resources are implemented with the appropriate and updated software to prevent a computer virus infection.
- Develops security solutions for the company's networks and virtual private networks, key public infrastructures, authentication and directory services, ensuring the security of unauthorized access.
- Works closely with the business unit's information systems teams to ensure that they are complying with the security baseline, and to mitigate virus risks to the enterprise.
- Ensures the company's strategic platforms are compliant to security policy by performing periodic scans against policy settings.
- Accountable for performing periodic scans of networks to identify security vulnerabilities and provides remediation alternatives.
- Oversees the application and administration of security policy on network-attached resources.
- Develops security solutions that require resolution of extremely complex operational and integration issues to successfully deploy secure technologies.
- Works with vendors, external organizations or customers to define security requirements and identify project opportunities.

Qualification Guidelines: Master's degree in computer science or other studies relevant to this position and more than six years of experience with a major corporation and/or law enforcement, intelligence, or public or private sector security organization, or bachelor's degree in computer science or other studies relevant to this position and more than 10 years of experience with a major law enforcement, intelligence, or public or private sector security organization. Some exposure in the international security arena is desirable. Certified Information Systems Security Professional (CISSP) preferred.

Senior Network Security Specialist IV
Job Description:

- Works under consultative direction toward predetermined goals and objectives.
- Assignments are usually self-initiated.
- Determines and pursues courses of action necessary to obtain desired results, and makes recommendations and changes to departmental policies and procedures.

- Work is checked through consultation and agreement, rather than formal review of supervisor.
- Responsible for the research, design, development, and implementation of extremely complex computer network security/protection technologies for company information and network systems/applications.
- Develops security plans, designs, best practices, and guidelines for existing or new technologies within network security and firewall protection.
- Develops virus protection security procedures to insure that email and email attachments are appropriately scanned and all network-attachment resources are implemented with the appropriate and updated software to prevent a computer virus infection.
- Provide security solutions for the company's networks and virtual private networks, key public infrastructures, authentication and directory services, ensuring the security of unauthorized access.
- Performs periodic scans of networks to identify security vulnerabilities and provide remediation alternatives.
- Conduct security risk assessment to ensure compliance with corporate security policies and adherence to best practices.
- Develops security design plans to implement, test, and manage new or existing network security technologies and strategies.
- Provides security solutions that require resolution of complex operational and integration issues to successfully deploy secure technologies.
- Serves on internal committees to represent and support computer/Internet security interests.
- Works with vendors, external organizations, or customers to define security requirements and identify project opportunities.
- Provides leadership to less experienced Computer and Information Security Specialist and Technicians.
- May act as lead person or technical expert on large projects.

Qualification Guidelines: Master's degree in computer science or other studies relevant to this position and more than four years of experience with a major corporation and/or law enforcement, intelligence, or public or private sector security organization, or bachelor's degree in computer science or other studies relevant to this position and more than eight years of experience with a major corporation and/or law enforcement, intelligence, or public or private sector security organization. Exposure in the international security arena is desirable. Certified Information Systems Security Professional (CISSP) preferred.

Network Security Specialist III

Job Description: Works under very limited direction in determining computer and information security techniques to accomplish objectives.

- Work is reviewed upon completion for adequacy in meeting objectives.
- Researches, designs, develops, and implements computer network security/protection technologies for the organization's information and network systems/applications.
- Develops, implements, and maintains extremely complex network and firewall security plans and configurations based on security requirements, project schedules, network topologies, applications and security standards.
- May develop security solutions for company networks, virtual private networks and public key infrastructure, authentication, and directory services, ensuring security vulnerabilities and providing remediation alternatives.
- Conducts security assessments and vulnerabilities analysis studies of existing network to verify policies are maintained.
- Works with senior specialists to apply and administer virus protection security to insure that email and email attachments are appropriately scanned and all network-attachment resources are implemented with appropriate and updated software to provide computer virus protection.
- Assist in the development and planning to detect and assess threats as well as acquire and distribute virus protection software.
- Provides forecasts of all work order activity including trouble ticket quantities and workload estimates to security fix agencies, vendors, and downstream organizations.
- Provides oversight to the client group on appropriate procedures for network computer/system security.
- Performs periodic scans of networks to identify security vulnerabilities and provides remediation alternatives.
- Provides leadership to less experienced Computer and Information Security Specialist and Technicians.

- May act as lead person or technical expert on medium to large projects.

Qualification Guidelines: Master's degree in computer science or other studies relevant to this position and more than three years of experience with a major corporation and/or law enforcement, intelligence, or public or private sector security organization, or bachelor's degree in computer science or other studies relevant to this position and more than six years of experience with a major corporation and/or law enforcement, intelligence, or public or private sector security organization. Some exposure in the international security arena is desirable. Certified Information Systems Security Professional (CISSP) preferred.

Network Security Specialist II
Job Description:

- Works is performed under general supervision. Follows established procedures.
- Work is reviewed systematically through completion for adequacy in meeting objectives.
- With guidance, conducts research, design, development, and implementation of computer network security and protection technologies for organization's information and network systems/applications.
- Develops, implements, and maintains complex network and firewall security plans and configurations based on security requirements, project schedules, network topologies, applications, and security standards.
- May develop security solutions for company networks, virtual private networks and public key infrastructure, authentication, and directory services, ensuring security vulnerabilities and providing remediation alternatives.
- Assists senior specialist in developing security standards and best practices.
- Works with senior specialist to administer virus protection security to ensure that email and email attachments are appropriately scanned and all network-attachment resources are implemented with appropriate and updated software to provide computer virus protection.
- Assists in the development and planning to detect and assess threats as well as acquire and distribute virus protection software.

- Provides forecasts of all work order activity including trouble ticket quantities and workload estimates to downstream organizations.
- Performs periodic scans of networks to identify security vulnerabilities and provides remediation alternatives.
- Reviews network security assessment and vulnerability analysis information to incorporate changes in common practices.
- Assists in security site surveys.
- Works to ensure that all email and email attachments are appropriately scanned and all network-attached resources are implemented with appropriate and updated software within assigned support group, to prevent computer virus infection.
- Acts as alternate team lead on small computer security incidents. Conducts technical evaluations of hardware, software, and installed systems and networks.
- Conducts certification testing of installed systems to ensure protection strategies are properly implemented.

Qualification Guidelines: Bachelor's degree in computer science or other studies relevant to this position and more than four years of experience in corporate security and/or law enforcement, intelligence, or public or private sector security organization. Certified Information Systems Security Professional (CISSP) preferred.

Network Security Specialist I
Job Description:

- Works under close supervision.
- Performs tasks from detailed instructions and established procedures.
- Work is reviewed for soundness of technical judgment and for following the defined policies and procedures.
- Under direction of senior staff, evaluates, designs, and develops computer network security/protection technologies for company information and network systems/applications.
- May assist in the implementation, development, and maintenance of moderately complex network and firewall security plans and configurations based on security requirements, project schedules, network topologies, applications, and security standards.
- Assists senior specialist to develop security solutions for company networks, virtual private networks and public key infrastructure,

authentication, and directory services, ensuring security vulnerabilities and providing remediation alternatives.

- Evaluates network security reports and studies to assist in the identification and resolution of potential security vulnerabilities and suspicious activities.
- Adheres to current security engineering practices, best practices, and standards.
- Assists in the administration of virus protection security to ensure that email and email attachments are appropriately scanned and all network-attachment resources are implemented with appropriate and updated software to provide computer virus protection.
- Performs periodic scans of networks to identify security vulnerabilities and recommends remediation alternatives. Assists in security site surveys.
- Conducts routine testing of installed systems to ensure protection strategies are properly implemented.

Qualification Guidelines: Bachelor's degree in computer science or other studies relevant to this position and a minimum of two years of experience in corporate security and/or law enforcement, intelligence, or public or private sector security organization.

Manager, Security Systems and Training

Job Description: Plans and directs the organization's security computer systems, data repositories, and technology tools under senior management direction.

- Implements technology solutions and services for security website, personnel identification, incident reporting, case management, and system validation.
- Serves as leading technical expert on complex security equipment and techniques.
- Oversees technical functions in support of security and investigative operations.
- Directs the evaluation of state of the art products and techniques related to computer hardware and software. Provides expertise of their use, recommends equipment, and adapts changes to computer technologies.
- Provides technical advice, guidance, and recommendations regarding security programs and awareness media.

- Implements staff, employee, and facility training programs; coordinates and develops communication plans, documented guidelines/manuals, and customer satisfaction surveys.
- Designs communication plans by documenting guidelines, brochures, surveys in on-line networks, and automated self-assessment formats.
- Acquires and coordinates training programs by adapting or translating materials from a variety of recognized sources.
- Analyzes departmental financial performance results and prepares expense and capital budget worksheets.
- Ensures successful program results and value contributions through interpersonal contact with peers and senior management.
- Manages the activities of and provides leadership direction to the professional, technical, and support staff within the organization unit.

Qualification Guidelines: Bachelor's degree in computer science or other studies relevant to this position and more than 10 years of experience with a major law enforcement, intelligence, or public or private sector security organization. Has had some exposure in the international security arena. Certified Information Systems Security Professional (CISSP) preferred and Certified Security Training Specialist (CSTS) preferred.

Senior Security Training and Awareness Specialist IV
Job Description:

- Works under consultative direction toward predetermined goals and objectives.
- Assignments are usually self-initiated. Determines and pursues courses of action necessary to obtain desired results, and makes recommendations and changes to departmental policies and procedures.
- Work is checked through consultation and agreement, rather than formal review by supervisor.
- Acts as a senior member of a team to implement technology solutions and services for security website, personnel identification, incident reporting, case management, and system validation.
- Administers presentation of initial or new hire security briefing, annual refresher, and termination briefings for the organization.

- Accountable for automated administrative system to ensure tracking of briefing attendance.
- Employs a variety of awareness media to keep managers and employees abreast of latest information, personnel, and technical security policies, procedures, trends, and issues.
- Communicates with line and staff personnel on potential threats to work environment.
- Through appropriate media devices, ensures line and staff personnel are kept abreast of potential threats, vulnerabilities, and counter-measures germane to work environment.
- Participates in local, regional, and national workshops and seminars related to security education and awareness.
- Keeps abreast of hardware and software security applications and their use in the current operating environment.
- Provides input for the development of new security-related orders, manuals, and guides and delivers presentations to organization staff.
- Provides leadership to less experienced security awareness/training specialists and technicians.

Qualification Guidelines: Bachelor's degree in an area of study relevant to this position and more than eight years of experience in emergency management with a law enforcement or public or private sector security organization. Certified Security Training Specialist (CSTS) preferred.

Security Training and Awareness Specialist III
Job Description:

- Works under very general direction.
- Exercises reasonable latitude in determining security communication/awareness techniques to accomplish objectives.
- Work is reviewed upon completion for adequacy in meeting objectives.
- Works as a team member to implement technology solutions and services for security website, personnel identification, incident reporting, case management, and system validation.
- Administers presentation of initial or new hire security briefing, annual refresher, and termination briefings for the organization.
- Accountable for automated administrative system to ensure tracking of briefing attendance. Employs a variety of awareness media to

keep managers and employees abreast of latest information, personnel, and technical security policies, procedures, trends, and issues.

- Communicates with line and staff personnel on potential threats to work environment.
- Through appropriate media devices, ensures line and staff personnel are kept abreast of potential threats, vulnerabilities, and countermeasures germane to work environment.
- Participates in local, regional, and national workshops and seminars related to security education and awareness.
- Keeps abreast of hardware and software security applications and their use in the current operating environment.
- Provides input for the development of new security-related orders, manuals, and guides and delivers presentations to organization staff.
- Provides leadership to less experienced security awareness/training specialists and technicians.

Qualification Guidelines: Bachelor's degree in an area of study relevant to this position and more than six years of experience in emergency management with a law enforcement or public or private sector security organization. Certified Security Training Specialist (CSTS) preferred.

Manager, Regulatory Compliance

Job Description: Plans and directs the business compliance function for the total corporation under senior management direction based on predetermined goals and objectives.

- Provides corporate-wide focus for efforts relating to compliance with government procurement laws and regulations and with the organization's policies on business ethics and conduct in contracting with government agencies, including oversight responsibility for government contract compliance audit and training functions.
- Works with various functions within the corporation to establish policy on a variety of procurement matters, including government accounting, government property, and independent research and development issues.
- Provides guidance and expertise in the development and maintenance of the company's compliance risk management program to assess, prioritize, and manage legal and regulatory compliance risks based on benchmarking research, thereby facilitating the systematic assessment and management of compliance risks.

- Maintains an expertise on government procurement laws.
- Reviews corporate policies, systems, and procedures with respect to procurement matters and assists in drafting such policies to ensure that they establish a level of conduct that complies with applicable laws.
- Provides oversight and coordination for government contract training, policy, and related relationships within operating units and external organizations including suppliers.
- Conducts internal reviews to evaluate effectiveness of compliance efforts and to identify deficiencies in meeting the organization's expectations in its procurement practices.
- Interacts with government agencies in the conduct of investigations and audits on procurement/commercial matters.
- Has a thorough knowledge of the corporation's business strategies, policies, standards, and practices.
- Manages responsibilities within approved budget. In fulfilling these responsibilities, the incumbent must work closely with staff functions, including: Government Contract Compliance Audit, Internal Audit, Finance, Legal, and Human Resources.

Qualification Guidelines: J.D. or master's degree and more than five years of experience or bachelor's degree and more than eight years of experience. Work experience should include a minimum of three years of management responsibility and five years or more relevant work in domestic and international government regulatory compliance and laws.

Measurement in Information Protection

WHAT'S HERE

This appendix offers some recommended approaches to developing measurement programs to improve information protection efforts.

HOW TO USE THIS APPENDIX

Consider the measurements included in this Appendix within the context of your organization.

INITIAL MEASUREMENT PROGRAM

Many organizations are able to develop procedures to collect information from currently available sources for consolidated presentation to management. This will often include:

1. Financial reporting—a summary of financial reporting audit activity and responses:
   A. Number of audit exceptions reported this period
   B. Number of audit findings closed this period
   C. Number of audit findings outstanding at end of period
2. High value asset monitoring—when available from log analysis or file-based controls:
   A. Number of protected directories monitored at period end
   B. Number of high-value files monitored at period end
   C. Total number of access attempts during period of report
   D. Number of authorized file accesses allowed
   E. Number of unauthorized file access attempts disallowed
3. Malware interdiction coverage—the performance of currently operational controls such as email filtering and malware control products:
   A. Number of email messages processed this period
   B. Inbound email:
      i. Inbound email with observed spam
      ii. Inbound email with observed malware

C. Outbound email:
  iii. Outbound email with observed spam
  iv. Outbound email with observed malware
4. IP program coverage—reporting on the state of information assurance policy adoption and dissemination:
  A. Percentage of IP program elements for which approved policies and controls are currently operational
  B. Percentage of staff who are assigned responsibilities for information security policies and controls and who have acknowledged accountability for their responsibilities in connection with those policies and controls
  C. Percentage of information security policy compliance reviews with no violations noted
  D. Percentage of position descriptions that define the information security roles, responsibilities, and skills
  E. Percentage of job performance reviews that include evaluation of information security responsibilities and information security policy compliance
  F. Percentage of user roles, systems, and applications that comply with the separation of duties principle
5. Business conduct incidents—reporting on the business conduct incidents:
  A. Number of new incidents during period
  B. Number of incident cases closed in period
  C. Number of incident cases open at period end
6. Pre-hire background coverage—reporting on number and nature of background checks:
  A. Number of new hires in period
  B. Number of new hires that were subject to background verification
  C. Number of new hires who completed psychological evaluation
7. Systems patch coverage—reporting on current patch state of IT systems:
  A. Number of server-grade systems in service:
    i. Number of systems at current patch level
    ii. Number of systems behind current patch level
  B. Number of client-grade systems in service:
    i. Number of systems at current patch level
    ii. Number of systems behind current patch level

8. Compliance audit performance—summary of compliance audits:
   A. Number of compliance exceptions resolved this period
   B. Number of compliance exceptions outstanding at period end

EVOLUTIONARY PROCESS IMPROVEMENT

As additional control systems are implemented within the IP program, the analysis of their performance by using measurements will enable enhancement of the ongoing threat reporting capability. Some of the examples of extended and enhanced controls are:

1. Monitoring of identified employee or agent communications
2. Enhanced monitoring of new hires and terminating employees communications
3. Internet monitoring of social media and public venues for organization image and data protection
4. Network intrusion monitoring for capable locations—reports from log analysis of host-based and network-based intrusion detection and prevention systems at such time as they are implemented
5. Monitoring network for exfiltration and advanced persistent threats (data protection)—reports from APT/data protection systems at such time as they are implemented
6. Security training and awareness:
   A. Reporting of security training and awareness activities:
      i. Percentage of new employees hired this reporting period who satisfactorily completed security awareness training before being granted network access
      ii. Percentage of employees who have satisfactorily completed periodic security awareness refresher training as required by policy
   B. By business unit:
      i. Percentage of employees and contractors aware of information protection policy
      ii. Percentage of employees and contractors aware of confidential reporting policy
      iii. Percentage of employees and contractors aware of safe workplace policy
      iv. Percentage of employees and contractors aware of Internet use policy

7. Business continuity coverage—as development of contingency planning process occurs, most of these measures will be available based on the program development progress. Once contingency planning is fully operational, some measures will no longer be material, and others will then be based on ongoing contingency planning program activities:
   A. Percent of company operational units operating under a complete tested contingency plan
   B. Percent of critical business functions operating under a complete tested contingency plan
   C. Number of contingent incidents reported:
      i. Number of incidents where recovery was within the established time objective
      ii. Number of incident where impact conformed to the established recovery objective
   D. Reported by criticality of business functions:
      i. The number or percentage of plans tested (walk through, actual, table top, call test, other)
      ii. The number or percentage of critical business functions tested at alternate sites
   E. The number of critical business functions' covered by contingent alternate seats (by location):
      i. Seats required vs. available and ready
   F. Outage causes by location
   G. Cost of business continuity operations per capita
   H. Cost of business continuity operations compared to cost of downtime to business interruption
   I. Percentage of business units owning highly critical business processes demonstrates fully competent business continuity planners
8. Risk management summary—upon development of a risk management process, it will be possible to report based on audit results, incident reports, and management initiatives:
   A. Number of confirmed vulnerabilities added (total, high, medium, and low risk)
   B. Number of vulnerabilities remediated (total, high, medium, and low risk)
   C. Number of vulnerabilities unresolved at period end (total, high, medium, and low risk)

Boran Consulting, "Information Classification," http://www.boran.com/security/IT1x-4.html.

Carnegie Mellon Software Engineering Institute, *Handbook for Computer Security Incident Response Teams (CSIRTs)*, April 2003, http://www.cert.org/archive/pdf/csirt-handbook.pdf.

Department of Information Resources for the State of Texas, http://www.dir.state.tx.us/security/policy/Pages/policy.aspx.

International Organization for Standardization (ISO) 27002:2005, "Information Technology – Security Techniques – Code of Practice for Information Security Management," http://www.iso.org/iso/catalogue_detail?csnumber = 50297.

Information Systems Audit and Control Association (ISACA), http://www.isaca.org/.

National Center for Education Statistics, *On-Site Inspection Guideline*, http://nces.ed.gov/statprog/rudman/k.asp.

National Institute of Standards and Technology (NIST), "Contingency Planning Guide for Federal Information Systems," SP 800-34, Rev. 1, May 2010, http://csrc.nist.gov/publications/nistpubs/800-34-rev1/sp800-34-rev1_errata-Nov11-2010.pdf.

National Institute of Standards and Technology (NIST), "Building an Information Technology Security Awareness and Training Program," SP 800-50, October 2003, http://csrc.nist.gov/publications/nistpubs/800-50/NIST-SP800-50.pdf.

National Institute of Standards and Technology (NIST), "Computer Security Incident Handling Guide," SP 800-61, Rev. 2, August 2012, http://csrc.nist.gov/publications/nistpubs/800-61rev2/SP800-61rev2.pdf.

National Institute of Standards and Technology (NIST), "Guide to Malware Incident Prevention and Handling for Desktops and

Laptops," SP 800-83, Rev. 1, July 2013, http://nvlpubs.nist.gov/nist-pubs/SpecialPublications/NIST.SP.800-83r1.pdf.

National Institute of Standards and Technology (NIST), "Information Security Handbook: A Guide for Managers SP 800-100," October 2006, http://csrc.nist.gov/publications/nistpubs/800-100/SP800-100-Mar07-2007.pdf.

National Security Institute (NSI), Improving Security from the Inside Out: A Business Case for Corporate Security Awareness, 2009, http://www.nsi.org/lc-free-reports.html.

Open Directory Project, Sample Information Protection Policies, http://dmoz.org/Computers/Security/Policy/Sample_Policies/.

Ruskwig,"Security Policies: ISO 27002 – ISO 27001 – ISO 17799," http://www.ruskwig.com/security_policies.htm.

Rutgers University, Office of Information Technology, http://ruse-cure.rutgers.edu/.

The UK Department for Business Innovation and Skills, *Security Policy Framework*, April 2013, https://www.gov.uk/government/publications/security-policy-framework.

The University of Texas Health Science Center at Houston (UTHealth), "Roles and Responsibilities for University Information Resources," http://www.uthouston.edu/hoop/policy.htm?id = 1448198.

The SANS Institute, "Information Security Policy Templates," http://www.sans.org/security-resources/policies/.

Treasury Board of Canada, "Audit of Business Continuity Planning," http://www.tbs-sct.gc.ca/report/orp/2012/abcp-vpca/abcp-vpca00-eng.asp.

REFERENCES

McAfee Labs. McAfee threats report: First quarter 2012. (2012). <http://www.mcafee.com/us/resources/reports/rp-quarterly-threat-q1-2012.pdf>.

Symantec Corporation. Internet security threat report 2013. (April, 2013). <http://www.symantec.com/security_response/publications/threatreport.jsp>.

Greg Kane has held a director role for the Security Executive Council for more than seven years. In this role he is responsible for mitigating risk as it applies to IT systems and the extensive intellectual property assets contained within. He has been responsible for disaster recovery and business continuity for various organizations for over 20 years. His work experience also includes analysis of security-related regulations, standards, and guidelines in order to encourage efficient and value-added compliance management. Greg leverages his strong skills in research and analysis to write a monthly security newsletter published to an audience of over 10,000 security practitioners. Before joining his current employer, Greg provided services to multiple businesses from retail to high-tech manufacturing. This included over ten successful years with a leading international business consulting services provider. Greg's educational background includes an MS degree in computer science and an MBA.

Lorna Koppel has been the VP, chief information security officer (CISO) for Iron Mountain since January 2013. Her role is designed to bring focus to growing information security (IS) needs and to deliver an effective global IS program to protect Iron Mountain's proprietary and confidential information, customer information, and technology infrastructure.

Her key responsibilities at Iron Mountain include overseeing IS governance, including global policies, standards, and the technology architecture strategy; assessing and managing IS compliance and assurance needs for Iron Mountain's customers; and overseeing the Computer Incident Response Center, technology risk assessments, and risk management processes.

Lorna has an extensive background in IS with over 20 years of experience in security and systems administration, risk analysis, and the implementation of high-profile global strategic initiatives. Throughout her career, she has worked closely with senior leaders and cross-functional teams to develop and execute strategic and tactical security programs, and developed strategies to address regulatory compliance mandates and other security-related requirements.

Prior to joining Iron Mountain, Lorna was the CISO for global consumer goods manufacturer Kohler and director of global security at network service provider BT/Infonet Services Corp. She began her career as a meteorologist with the US Air Force and has degrees from Bowling Green State University, Penn State, and the State University of New York at Albany.

In November 2010 Lorna was recognized as one of the industry's "Most Influential People in Security" in the information technology/cyber security practitioners category by *Security* magazine.

ABOUT ELSEVIER'S SECURITY EXECUTIVE COUNCIL RISK MANAGEMENT PORTFOLIO

Elsevier's Security Executive Council Risk Management Portfolio is the voice of the security leader. It equips executives, practitioners, and educators with research-based, proven information and practical solutions for successful security and risk management programs. This portfolio covers topics in the areas of risk mitigation and assessment, ideation and implementation, and professional development. It brings trusted operational research, risk management advice, tactics, and tools to business professionals. Previously available only to the Security Executive Council community, this content—covering corporate security, enterprise crisis management, global IT security, and more—provides real-world solutions and "how-to" applications. This portfolio enables business and security executives, security practitioners, and educators to implement new physical and digital risk management strategies and build successful security and risk management programs.

Elsevier's Security Executive Council Risk Management Portfolio is a key part of the **Elsevier Risk Management & Security Collection**. The collection provides a complete portfolio of titles for the business executive, practitioner, and educator by bringing together the best imprints in risk management, security leadership, digital forensics, IT security, physical security, homeland security, and emergency management: Syngress, which provides cutting-edge computer and information security material; Butterworth-Heinemann, the premier security, risk management, homeland security, and disaster-preparedness publisher; and Anderson Publishing, a leader in criminal justice publishing for more than 40 years. These imprints, along with the addition of Security Executive Council content, bring the work of highly regarded authors into one prestigious, complete collection.

The Security Executive Council (www.securityexecutivecouncil.com) is a leading problem-solving research and services organization focused on helping businesses build value while improving their ability to effectively manage and mitigate risk. Drawing on the collective knowledge of a large community of successful security practitioners, experts, and strategic alliance partners, the Council develops strategy and insight and identifies proven practices that cannot be found anywhere else.

Their research, services, and tools are focused on protecting people, brand, information, physical assets, and the bottom line.

Elsevier (www.elsevier.com) is an international multimedia publishing company that provides world-class information and innovative solutions tools. It is part of Reed Elsevier, a world-leading provider of professional information solutions in the science, medical, risk, legal, and business sectors.

Printed and bound by CPI Group (UK) Ltd, Croydon, CR0 4YY

03/10/2024

01040423-0011